Author: Tiffany Townsend
Cover/Logo Design: Camilla Acosta
Production: Lamont Townsend

ISBN 978-0-9891327-3-2

P.O. Box 1155 Snellville, GA 30078 | www.3idpublishing.com

3id Publishing exists to intrigue children to explore God and all of His wonders through creative and inspired literary works, instruction and presentation. It is the vision of 3id Publishing to inspire children to want to learn more about God; to ignite the hearts of God's children with a passion for an authentic relationship with Jesus Christ, laying the foundation for every child to find his/her identity in God.

Email info@3idpublishing.com to book the 3id Publishing Team for a consult/training.

Nursery/Preschool Bible Curriculum

Planting God's Word into children one seed at at time.

Apple Seeds Kidz is a nursery and preschool Bible curriculum. The primary objective of Apple Seeds Kidz is to provide quality, creative, and innovative children's ministry at an affordable price. The suggested props that accompany each lesson are either household items, or materials that are inexpensive enough to fit within even the smallest budget.

Lessons are provided for the following age groups:

Babies (Birth - 12 Months)
One Year Olds (12-24 Months)
Two & Three Year Olds
Four & Five Year Olds

In addition, Apple Seeds Kidz provides all original songs to enhance lessons and make children's ministry engaging.

It is our prayer that children will grow in the knowledge of the love, grace, and sacrifice of our Lord and Savior Jesus Christ. We pray that children experience the love of Christ through every lesson, story, activity, and song. It is our mission that children would discover their true and unique identity in God and move passionately into the perfect will of God for their lives.

WHAT'S INSIDE?

Each volume of Apple Seeds contains three series of lessons. In this first volume, your babies and preschoolers will discover how they can be Just Like Jesus. Lesson series include the following:

Lesson Plans
Bible Blast Story Cards
Parent Pacts
Scripture Seed Cards
Activity Pages

1 Kind Like Jesus pages 9-31

Children discover how they can be kind the way that Jesus is kind. Each of these lessons will teach children all the many ways that we can demonstrate God's loving kindness.

2 Forgive Like Jesus pages 32-54

Forgiveness is not always easy, even for adults. Use this lesson series to show your preschoolers how we can forgive the way that Jesus forgives us. *For Babies and 1 Year Olds, this lesson series is Love Like Jesus.

3 Obey Like Jesus pages 55-82

During this lesson series, children will learn how God wants us to obey the way that Jesus obeyed God. These lessons will teach children that every act of obedience is an act of love.

SLICING INTO APPLE SEEDS

Apple Seeds Kidz lessons are divided into different segments that can be incorporated into any service schedule. Listed below is an outline of the segments found in each lesson.

Core Concept

The general concept being conveyed over the lesson series.

Scripture Seed

The focal scripture for the lesson series.

Life Lesson

The practical application of the scripture seed and the core concept.

Apples to Apples

Apples to Apples is a time for activities that will reinforce the Bible Blast, core concept, and the life lesson. You can use this activity to help your children connect to the Bible at their level.

Transition Song

Use this song to transition between activities to reinforce the core concept.

Bible Blast

Engaging and interactive Bible story.

Tree Chat

Use this time to allow children to discuss life happenings that they are excited about. Tree Chat is designed to give children an opportunity to say what's on their minds, so that they can fully engage in the lesson activities further into the service.

Apple-tizer

The Apple-tizer is an introduction to the Bible Blast lesson that is usually delivered in the form of a game, song, or structured activity.

Bible Bites

Bible Bites is the monthly core concept activity that can be done during snack time. Use Bible Bites to reinforce the core concept.

Life Lesson Review

Complete the Life Lesson Review as a dismissal activity so that children remain engaged upon parent arrival. Use this time to reinforce the life lesson.

Bye-Bye Baby

Complete Bye-Bye Baby at the end of service to recap the core concept.

Bye-Bye Bible Review

Complete the Bye-Bye Bible Review as a dismissal activity so that children remain engaged upon parent arrival.

LESSON PLANS

Let's Talk Apples!

Talk with your babies about how kind Jesus is. Take every opportunity to express Jesus' loving kindness to your precious little ones.

Transition Song

I am kind, I am kind,
I am kind like
JESUS!

I am kind, I am kind,
I am kind like
JESUS!

I am kind, I am kind,
I am kind like
JESUS!

I am kind just like
you GOD!

Core Concept
I can be kind like Jesus.

Scripture Seed
Always try to be kind to each other and to everyone else.
-1 Thessalonians 5:15 (NIrV)

Sing the following chant with your babies during diaper changes, feedings, and play time:

Wherever I look *(put your hands over your eyes)*
I wll find *(take your hands off of your eyes)*
Jesus is kind, *(smile)*
All the time! *(touch baby's nose)*

Let's Talk Apples!

In this lesson, your tiny friends will learn what it means to be kind just like Jesus! Take every opportunity to express Jesus' loving kindness to your toddlers.

Core Concept
I can be kind like Jesus.

Scripture Seed
Always try to be kind to each other and to everyone else.
-1 Thessalonians 5:15 (NIrV)

Transition Song

I am kind, I am kind
I am kind like JESUS!

I am kind, I am kind
I am kind like JESUS!

I am kind, I am kind
I am kind like JESUS!

I am kind just like
you GOD!

Lesson Supplies

-play food
-basket
-look-through tube (can use toilet paper/
 paper towel rolls, etc.)
-bells
-stuffed teddy bear

Bible Blast
Good Helper

Supplies: play food, basket

Do this: Sit your toddlers close to you on the floor. Scatter the play food on the floor. Have the children help you put all the food back into the basket.

Say this: "Oh my! I've dropped all of my food on the floor. Can you help me put my food back in the basket? You are all so kind! Jesus is kind too!"

Apples to Apples
Soooo Kind!

Do this: Gather children close to you either on the floor or seated at tables. Go around to each child and pat them on the head while counting to three.

Say this: On the third child, say – "(child's name) is sooo kind… just like Jesus!"

Repeat with all children.

Kind Bells
Supplies: bells

Do this: Ring the bells and sing the kind bells chant. Repeat with all children.

Say this: "I see (child's name)! God made (child's name) very special!

Kind bells are ringing,
We are singing
Jesus is kind
All the time!
Repeat with children's names.

Bible Bites
I See Kindness

Supplies: look-through tube

Do this: Sit children at the table or on the floor in a circle for snack time. Use the look-through tube to look at the children and call out specific descriptors about each child (ie. red shirt, brown hair, etc.)

Say this: "I see someone wearing a blue shirt, with brown hair. I see that (child's name) is kind just like Jesus!"

Bye-Bye Baby
Share Bear

Supplies: teddy bear

Do this: Sit children close to you on the floor. Talk about your special toy. Give the teddy bear a big hug. Pass the teddy bear around to the children and allow each child a chance to hug the bear.

Say this: "I really like my teddy bear. I want to be kind like Jesus is kind so I am going to share my toy with all of you. Would you like to give him a hug too? Wow, you are all so kind!"

Let's Talk Apples!

Your 2 & 3 year old toddlers will have a blast discovering how they can be just like Jesus! This lesson series is filled with fun stories and activities that will show your little ones how they can be kind like Jesus.

Core Concept
I can be kind like Jesus.

Scripture Seed
Always try to be kind to each other and to everyone else.
-1 Thessalonians 5:15 (NIrV)

Transition Song

I am kind, I am kind
I am kind like JESUS!

I am kind, I am kind
I am kind like JESUS!

I am kind, I am kind
I am kind like JESUS!

I am kind just like
you GOD!

A Very Kind Man

Lesson Supplies

-Bible Blast Story Card
-cupcake pan
-2 small envelopes
-baseball cap
-Kind Clock (found in activity pages

-Play coins
-basket
-upbeat music
-masking tape
-smiley face activity pages

Bible Blast
A Very Kind Man

Supplies: *Bible Blast story card, cupcake pan, 2 small envelopes, baseball cap*

Do this: Read the Bible Blast story. Use the cupcake pan, envelopes, and baseball cap as directed in the Bible story. Don't forget to reinforce the core concept.

Apples to Apples
Coin Toss

Supplies: *play coins, basket*

Do this: Have the children take turns tossing the coins into the basket. Recap what the Good Samaritan did with the coins from the Bible Blast story.

Smiley Freeze!

Supplies: *upbeat music, masking tape*

Do this: Make 2-3 big smiley faces with the masking tape on the floor. Play the music. Periodically stop the music. When the music stops, children should all get inside the smiley faces taped on the floor.

Say this: *"In our Bible story today, we learned about being kind. It makes God smile when we are kind to each other. When the music stops, I want everyone to jump inside the smiley faces!"*

Bible Bites
Kind All The Time

Supplies: *Kind Clock*

Do this: Use the Kind Clock and spin the hour hand as you sing the Kind All the Time chant.

Say this:

We are...
Kind at 1-2-3 o'clock
Kind at 4-5-6 o'clock
Kind at 7-8-9 o'clock
10,11,12 o'clock
Tick tock!
We are kind
all the time!

Bye-Bye Bible Review
Kind Corners

Supplies: *smiley face activity pages, tape*

Do this: Tape smiley face activity pages to the corners of the room. Gather children to the middle of the room. Call out various scenarios and ask the children if it is kind or unkind. If it is kind, have the children run to the kind corners in the room, then have them return to the center of the room and read another scenario. Recap the Bible story.

Say this: *"Is sharing our toys kind? Yes it is! Run to the kind corners! Ok, come back to me. What about loving our pets? Yes! That's kind too! Run to the kind corners! Wow, you guys are so kind! What about helping our moms and dads? Is that kind?..."*
Repeat while children remain engaged.

Let's Talk Apples!

Your 2 & 3 year old toddlers will have a blast discovering how they can be just like Jesus! This lesson series is filled with fun stories and activities that will show your little ones how they can be kind like Jesus.

Core Concept
I can be kind like Jesus.

Scripture Seed
Always try to be kind to each other and to everyone else.
-1 Thessalonians 5:15 (NIrV)

Transition Song

I am kind, I am kind
I am kind like JESUS!

I am kind, I am kind
I am kind like JESUS!

I am kind, I am kind
I am kind like JESUS!

I am kind just like
you GOD!

A Very Kind Lady

Lesson Supplies

-Bible Blast Story Card
-pennies in a jar
-heart cut-outs
-empty tissue box
-Kind Clock (found in activity pages)

-play coins
-handheld mirror

Bible Blast
A Very Kind Lady

Supplies: *Bible Blast story card, pennies in a jar*

Do this: Read the Bible Blast story. Use the pennies so children can see what the widow gave. Don't forget to reinforce the core concept.

Apples to Apples
Love Offering

Supplies: *heart cut-outs, empty tissue box*

Do this: Place the box on a table and use it as an offering box. Have the children take turns placing their hearts inside the offering box. Recap the Bible story.

One-Two!

Do this: Gather children to the center of the room. Call out various body parts that are in pairs of two. Have children do action movements with those parts.

Say this: "Count with me... 1-2! We have two... legs! Jump up and down on your two legs! Great jumping! We also have two hands. Clap your two hands together! Cool clapping! We even have two arms. Put your arms up really high. Wow, that's high! How many ears do we have? (whisper) Yup, two! Let me see your ears! In our Bible story today, how many coins did the kind lady have? (wait for children to answer) That's right... two! How many did she give away? (wait for response) She sure did! She gave both her coins away! Do you think she was kind like Jesus?..."

Bible Bites
Kind All The Time

Supplies: *Kind Clock*

Do this: Use the Kind Clock and spin the hour hand as you sing the Kind All the Time chant.

Say this:

We are...
Kind at 1-2-3 o'clock
Kind at 4-5-6 o'clock
Kind at 7-8-9 o'clock
10,11,12 o'clock
Tick tock!
We are kind
all the time!

Bye-Bye Bible Review
One of a Kind

Supplies: *Hand-held mirror*

Do this: Gather children in a circle on the floor. Have children pass the mirror around to each other. As each child looks at him/herself in the mirror, repeat the One of a Kind chant.

Say this:

(child's name) is one of a kind
(child's name) is oh so kind!

Let's Talk Apples!

Your 2 & 3 year old toddlers will have a blast discovering how they can be just like Jesus! This lesson series is filled with fun stories and activities that will show your little ones how they can be kind like Jesus.

Core Concept
I can be kind like Jesus.

Scripture Seed
Always try to be kind to each other and to everyone else.
-1 Thessalonians 5:15 (NIrV)

Transition Song

I am kind, I am kind
I am kind like JESUS!

I am kind, I am kind
I am kind like JESUS!

I am kind, I am kind
I am kind like JESUS!

I am kind just like
you GOD!

Very Kind Friends

Lesson Supplies

-Bible Blast Story Card
-plastic cup
-long stick (limbo stick)
-upbeat music
-Kind Clock (found in activity pages)

Bible Blast
Very Kind Friends

Supplies: *Bible Blast story card, plastic cup with bottom cut out (can use empty paper towel or toilet tissue roll)*

Do this: Read the Bible Blast story. Use the cup and stick your hand through the opening to show how they cut a hole through the roof. Don't forget to reinforce the core concept.

Apples to Apples
All Kinds of Kind Friends

Do this: *Have children pretend to be different kinds of animals.*

Say this: "It's great to be kind friends! Let's pretend to be kind animal friends. Can you be a kind bunny friend? Let me see my kind bunnies hop! What about a kind lion friend? Let me hear you roar! How about a duck friend? Can you quack like a duck friend? Cool quacking!"

Friend Limbo

Supplies: *long stick, upbeat music*

Do this: Gather children to the center of the room. Play upbeat music and have teachers hold the friendship limbo stick. Direct children to get down low to go under the stick.

Say this: "In our Bible story today, the man's friends had to lower him down really low into the house so that he could get to Jesus. Can you get down really low? Get down really low to get under the friendship stick!"

Bible Bites
Kind All The Time

Supplies: Kind Clock

Do this: Use the Kind Clock and spin the hour hand as you sing the Kind All the Time chant.

Say this:
We are...
Kind at 1-2-3 o'clock
Kind at 4-5-6 o'clock
Kind at 7-8-9 o'clock
10,11,12 o'clock
Tick tock!
We are kind
all the time!

Bye-Bye Bible Review
Little Legs

Do this: Have children come together in a group. Call out various actions that the children can do with their legs.

Say this: "Can your little legs... jump up and down... wiggle... skip? Can you stand on one little leg? How about the other little leg? Do you remember the man in our Bible story today? He couldn't move his legs..."

Let's Talk Apples!

Your 2 & 3 year old toddlers will have a blast discovering how they can be just like Jesus! This lesson series is filled with fun stories and activities that will show your little ones how they can be kind like Jesus.

Core Concept
I can be kind like Jesus.

Scripture Seed
Always try to be kind to each other and to everyone else.
-1 Thessalonians 5:15 (NIrV)

Transition Song

I am kind, I am kind
I am kind like JESUS!

I am kind, I am kind
I am kind like JESUS!

I am kind, I am kind
I am kind like JESUS!

I am kind just like
you GOD!

A Very Kind King

Lesson Supplies

-Bible Blast Story Card
-big dollar, little dollar (from activity pages)
-kind crown (from activity pages)
-star cut-outs (from activity pages)
-Kind Clock (from activity pages)
-bubbles

Bible Blast
A Very Kind King

Supplies: *Bible Blast story card, big dollar, little dollar*

Do this: Read the Bible Blast story. Use the dollars as you read the Bible Blast story. Don't forget to reinforce the core concept.

Apples to Apples
Crown of Kindness

Supplies: *kind crown cut-out (from activity pages)*

Do this: Gather children together on the floor. Have children take turns wearing the kind crown and repeating the core concept.

Kind Star

Supplies: *star cut-outs (from activity pages)*

Do this: Tape star cut-outs to the floor. Direct children to follow you as you step on the stars around the room.

Say this: "In our Bible story today, the King wanted his servant to be kind because He was kind to him. God wants us to be kind like Jesus. Let's all be stars and kind. Step on these kind stars with me!"

Bible Bites
Kind All The Time

Supplies: *Kind Clock*

Do this: Use the Kind Clock and spin the hour hand as you sing the Kind All the Time chant.

Say this:

> We are...
> Kind at 1-2-3 o'clock
> Kind at 4-5-6 o'clock
> Kind at 7-8-9 o'clock
> 10,11,12 o'clock
> Tick tock!
> We are kind
> all the time!

Bye-Bye Bible Review
Problem Pop

Supplies: *bubbles*

Do this: Have children come together in the center of the room. Blow bubbles and direct children to pop them.

Say this: "God is so kind that He pops all the bad things we do away – just like these bubbles! Can you help me pop all these problems?"

Let's Talk Apples!

Your 4 & 5 year old friends will have an exciting time discovering all the ways that they can be just like Jesus! This lesson series is filled with fun stories and activities that will show your children how they can be kind like Jesus!

Core Concept
I can be kind like Jesus.

Scripture Seed
Always try to be kind to each other and to everyone else.
-1 Thessalonians 5:15 (NIrV)

Transition Song

I am kind, I am kind
I am kind like JESUS!

I am kind, I am kind
I am kind like JESUS!

I am kind, I am kind
I am kind like JESUS!

I am kind just like
you GOD!

A Very Kind Man
Lesson Supplies

-Bible Blast Story Card
-large laminated tree
-toy apple
-cupcake pan
-2 small envelopes
-baseball cap

-Kind Clock (found in activity pages)
-play coins
-basket
-Band-Aids®
-posterboard

Apple-tizer
Coin Toss

Supplies: play coins, basket

Do this: Have the children take turns tossing the coins into the basket.

Say this: "Let's see if we can toss these coins into the offering basket. Ready? Great job! It's so kind to give to people. In our Bible Blast story today, we are going to learn about a man who was kind, just like all of you!"

Bible Blast
A Very Kind Man

Supplies: Bible Blast story card, cupcake pan, 2 small envelopes, baseball cap

Do this: Read the Bible Blast story. Use the cupcake pan, envelopes, and baseball cap as directed in the Bible story. Choose 3 children to volunteer to be the baker, mailman, and Good Samaritan. Don't forget to reinforce the core concept.

Apple Tree Chat

Supplies: large laminated tree poster, toy apple

Do this: Hang laminated tree on the wall. Have children sit with you next to the tree. Ask children if there is anything that they would like to share about something exciting that happened or is happening in their lives. Only the child with the apple is allowed to share.

Apples to Apples
Kangaroos & Monkeys

Do this: Gather children together and have them pretend to be kangaroos. Ask children various questions about things that are kind. When you say something that is kind, have children hop like kind kangaroos. When you say something that is not kind, have them make monkey sounds like mean monkeys. Ask children if it's better to be mean monkeys or kind kangaroos. Continue while children are engaged.

Say this: "Ok friends, we are going to play a game. We have two animals – kind kangaroos, and mean monkeys. If I say something that is kind, I want you to hop around like the kind kangaroos. If I say something that is mean, I want you to move around like mean monkeys. Everybody ready? Is sharing your toys kind or mean? Is praying for someone kind or mean? Is hitting our friends kind or mean?..."

Bible Bites
Kind All The Time

Supplies: *Kind Clock*

Do this: Have children help you figure out what time it is on the Kind Clock. Ask children if we can be kind at various times of the day.

Say this: *"What time is it on our Kind Clock? It is 10:00! Can we be kind at 10:00? (allow children to respond) Yes! We can be kind like Jesus! Now it's 2:00! Can we be kind at 2:00?..."*

Life Lesson Review
Band-Aid® Kind

Supplies: *Band-Aid® Kind Poster*

Do this: Get a small poster board and write the word kind with Band-Aids®. Have children decorate the poster board. Repeat the scripture seed as you hold up the Band-Aid® Kind poster and have children shout kind! Encourage children to repeat the scripture seed with you. Review the life lesson.

Life Lesson / I should be kind and help others.

Let's Talk Apples!

Your 4 & 5 year old friends will have an exciting time discovering all the ways that they can be just like Jesus! This lesson series is filled with fun stories and activities that will show your children how they can be kind like Jesus!

Core Concept
I can be kind like Jesus.

Scripture Seed
Always try to be kind to each other and to everyone else.
-1 Thessalonians 5:15 (NIrV)

Transition Song

I am kind, I am kind
I am kind like JESUS!

I am kind, I am kind
I am kind like JESUS!

I am kind, I am kind
I am kind like JESUS!

I am kind just like
you GOD!

A Very Kind Lady

Lesson Supplies

-Bible Blast Story Card
-empty pickle jar
-2 pennies
-large laminated tree
-toy apple
-Kind Clock (found in activity pages)

-heart-cut outs (found in activity pages)
-popsicle sticks
-smiley faces (found in activity pages)
-tape

Apple-tizer
Two Times!

Do this: Call out various motions for children to do two times.

Say this: "The number 2 is special in our Bible story today, so whenever I call out something, I want you to do it 2 times. Ready?! Jump ... turn around ... clap... hop on one leg ... pat your head ... Great job! In our Bible Blast story today, there was a lady who had only 2 coins. Let's find out what happened!"

Bible Blast
A Very Kind Lady

Supplies: *Bible Blast story card, empty pickle jar, 2 pennies*

Do this: Read the Bible Blast story. Use the empty tissue box and 2 pennies as directed in the story. Don't forget to reinforce the core concept.

Apple Tree Chat

Supplies: *large laminated tree poster, toy apple*

Do this: Hang laminated tree on the wall. Have children sit with you next to the tree. Ask children if there is anything that they would like to share about something exciting that happened or is happening in their lives. Only the child with the apple is allowed to share.

Apples to Apples
Kind Heart

Supplies: *heart cut-outs, popsicle sticks*

Do this: Cut out hearts and distribute them to children. Have children color/decorate their hearts. Once children are finished coloring, glue popsicle sticks onto the hearts to make a heart mask. Gather together on the floor and have children take turns saying something that they can do/say that is kind while holding up their heart mask.

Supplies: *Kind Clock*

Do this: Have children help you figure out what time it is on the Kind Clock. Ask children if we can be kind at various times of the day.

Say this: *"What time is it on our Kind Clock? It is 10:00! Can we be kind at 10:00? (allow children to respond) Yes! We can be kind like Jesus! Now it's 2:00! Can we be kind at 2:00?..."*

Life Lesson Review
Kind Corners

Supplies: *red, blue, yellow, and green smiley faces (Kind Corners activity pages)*

Do this: Tape smiley faces in the four corners of the room. Call out colors randomly and have children run to the corner of the color called out.

Say this:

> *Red corner – repeat the life lesson*
> *Blue corner – repeat the scripture seed*
> *Yellow corner – name some kind things*
> *Green corner – recap the Bible Blast story*

Life Lesson | I should be kind and help others.

Let's Talk Apples!

Your 4 & 5 year old friends will have an exciting time discovering all the ways that they can be just like Jesus! This lesson series is filled with fun stories and activities that will show your children how they can be kind like Jesus!

Transition Song

I am kind, I am kind
I am kind like JESUS!

I am kind, I am kind
I am kind like JESUS!

I am kind, I am kind
I am kind like JESUS!

I am kind just like
you GOD!

Core Concept
I can be kind like Jesus.

Scripture Seed
Always try to be kind to each other and to everyone else.
-1 Thessalonians 5:15 (NIrV)

Very Kind Friends

Lesson Supplies

-Bible Blast Story Card
-large laminated tree
-toy apple
-Kind Clock (found in activity pages)

-plastic cup or empty paper towel/toilet tissue roll
-long stick (limbo stick)
-upbeat music

Apple-tizer
Crabwalk Fun!

Do this: Divide children up into two groups. 2 children will compete at a time in the crabwalk race. Encourage the other children to cheer on their friends.

Say this: *"That was awesome crab walking! You know what? In our Bible Blast story today, there was a man who couldn't walk…."*

Bible Blast
Very Kind Friends

Supplies: *Bible Blast story card, plastic cup with bottom cut out (can use empty paper towel or toilet tissue roll)*

Do this: Read the Bible Blast story. Look through the cup to show how they couldn't see Jesus close up. Use the same cup and stick your hand through the opening to show how they cut a hole through the roof. Don't forget to reinforce the core concept.

Apple Tree Chat

Supplies: *large laminated tree poster, toy apple*

Do this: Hang laminated tree on the wall. Have children sit with you next to the tree. Ask children if there is anything that they would like to share about something exciting that happened or is happening in their lives. Only the child with the apple is allowed to share.

Apples to Apples
Friend Limbo

Supplies: *long stick, upbeat music*

Do this: Gather children to the center of the room. Play upbeat music and have teachers hold the friendship limbo stick. Direct children to get down low to go under the stick.

Say this: *"In our Bible story today, the man's friends had to lower him down really low into the house so that he could get to Jesus. Can you get down really low? Get down really low to get under the friendship stick!"*

Bible Bites
Kind All The Time

Supplies: *Kind Clock*

Do this: Have children help you figure out what time it is on the Kind Clock. Ask children if we can be kind at various times of the day.

Say this: *"What time is it on our Kind Clock? It is 10:00! Can we be kind at 10:00? (allow children to respond) Yes! We can be kind like Jesus! Now it's 2:00! Can we be kind at 2:00?..."*

Life Lesson Review
Shake, Shake, Freeze!

Say this:

Shake, shake
Freeze! (freeze)
Shake, shake
Freeze! (freeze)
Be kind and help each other
Shake, shake
Freeze! (freeze)

Hop, hop
Freeze! (freeze)
Hop, hop
Freeze! (freeze)
Be kind and help each other
Hop, hop
Freeze! (freeze)
*Repeat with, clap, skip, tap, etc.

Life Lesson ❳ **I should be kind and help others.**

Let's Talk Apples!

Your 4 & 5 year old friends will have an exciting time discovering all the ways that they can be just like Jesus! This lesson series is filled with fun stories and activities that will show your children how they can be kind like Jesus!

Core Concept
I can be kind like Jesus.

Scripture Seed
Always try to be kind to each other and to everyone else.
-1 Thessalonians 5:15 (NIrV)

Transition Song

I am kind, I am kind
I am kind like JESUS!

I am kind, I am kind
I am kind like JESUS!

I am kind, I am kind
I am kind like JESUS!

I am kind just like
you GOD!

A Very Kind King

Lesson Supplies

-Bible Blast Story Card
-big & little dollar (from activity pages)
-large laminated tree
-toy apple
-Kind Clock (found in activity pages)

-lots & little cards (from activity pages)
-masking tape
-kind crown (from activity pages)

Apple-tizer
Lots & Little

Supplies: *lots & little cards (from activity pages)*

Do this: Gather children together and go through the Lots & Little Cards. Ask children which is a lot and which is a little.

Say this: *"Awesome job everyone! In our Bible Blast story today, there was a man who owed lots and there was another man who owed a little..."*

Bible Blast
A Very Kind King

Supplies: *Bible Blast story card, big dollar, little dollar*

Do this: Read the Bible Blast story. Use the dollars as you read the Bible Blast story. Don't forget to reinforce the core concept.

Apple Tree Chat

Supplies: *large laminated tree poster, toy apple*

Do this: Hang laminated tree on the wall. Have children sit with you next to the tree. Ask children if there is anything that they would like to share about something exciting that happened or is happening in their lives. Only the child with the apple is allowed to share.

Apples to Apples
Circle of Kindness

Supplies: *Masking Tape*

Do this: Create 1-2 big circles on the floor with masking tape. Play upbeat music. Stop the music periodically. When the music stops, have children jump inside the circle of kindness and repeat the scripture seed. Restart the music and play again. Recap the Bible story.

Say this: *"In our Bible story today, was the King's servant inside or outside of the circle of kindness? Do we want to be inside or outside of the circle of kindness?..."*

Bible Bites
Kind All The Time

Supplies: Kind Clock

Do this: Have children help you figure out what time it is on the Kind Clock. Ask children if we can be kind at various times of the day.

Say this: "What time is it on our Kind Clock? It is 10:00! Can we be kind at 10:00? (allow children to respond) Yes! We can be kind like Jesus! Now it's 2:00! Can we be kind at 2:00?..."

Life Lesson Review
Crown of Kindness

Supplies: kind crown (from activity pages)

Do this: Gather children together on the floor. Have children take turns wearing the kind crown and repeating the life lesson.

Life Lesson / I should be kind and help others.

Let's Talk Apples!

Spend some time loving on your babies the way that God loves on us!

Core Concept
I can love like Jesus.

Scripture Seed
We love because he loved us first.
- 1 John 4:19 (NIrV)

Transition Song

I can love, I can love,
I can love like
JESUS!

I can love, I can love,
I can love like
JESUS!

I can love, I can love,
I can love like
JESUS!

I can love just like
you GOD!

Sing the following chant with your babies during diaper changes, feedings, and play time:

I can love and you can love (point to yourself and to baby) - Just like Jesus
I can love and you can love (point to yourself and to baby) - Just like Jesus
I can love and you can love (point to yourself and to baby) - Just like Jesus
God loves you and I do too!

Let's Talk Apples!

In this lesson, spend some time teaching your toddlers about what it means to love the way that Jesus loves.

Core Concept
I can love like Jesus.

Scripture Seed

We love because he loved us first.
- *1 John 4:19 (NIrV)*

Transition Song

I can love, I can love,
I can love like JESUS!

I can love, I can love,
I can love like JESUS!

I can love, I can love,
I can love like JESUS!

I can love just like
you GOD!

Lesson Supplies

-happy/sad face cards (from activity pages)
-Colors of Love Poster (from activity pages)
-smiley face stickers
-maracas (can make with beans and plastic
 easter eggs or fold over small paper plates
 placing beans inside, and staple plate)
-bubbles

Bible Blast
Upside Down Frown

Supplies: happy and sad face cards

Do this: Sit your toddlers close to you on the floor. Use the happy and sad face cards as you talk about what makes us happy and what makes us sad.

Say this: "Ok friends, has your friend or your brother or sister ever broken your toy? That might make you sad (hold up the sad face card). But Jesus wants us to forgive and love our friends the way that he forgives and loves us (hold up the happy face card).

Apples to Apples
Smile!

Supplies: smiley face stickers

Do this: Gather children close to you on the floor. Place a smiley face sticker on the hand of each child. (be aware of children that have allergies to adhesive)

Say this: "God wants us to forgive the way that he forgives us. He loves us so much and wants us to smile and love each other!"

Shake It Off

Supplies: maracas

Do this: shake the maracas as you sing the chant.

Say this:

Shake, shake, shake off your sad face
put, put, put on your happy face
Shake sadness away

Shake, shake, shake off your sad face
Put, put, put on your happy face

Love the Jesus way!

Bible Bites
Colors of Love

Supplies: Colors of Love Poster

Do this: Use the Colors of Love poster to show children all the shades of love. Sing the Colors of Love chant.

Say this:

Red and blue
I love you
yellow, green
I won't be mean
orange and purple
I am just so full
of love...for...YOU!

Bye-Bye Baby
Problem Pop

Supplies: bubbles

Do this: Gather children to an open area of the room. Have children help you pop all of the bubbles to show how Jesus forgives us and pops our mistakes away.

Say this: "Can you help me pop all these bubbles? Wow, that's great popping!"

Let's Talk Apples!

How amazing it is to learn that we can be just like Jesus! In this lesson series, your 2 & 3 year old toddler friends will have an opportunity to discover how they can Forgive Like Jesus!

Core Concept
I can forgive like Jesus.

Scripture Seed

Forgive each other, just as God forgave you because of what Christ has done.
-Ephesians 4:32 (NIrV)

Transition Song

I forgive, I forgive
I forgive like JESUS!

I forgive, I forgive
I forgive like JESUS!

I forgive, I forgive
I forgive like JESUS!

I forgive just like you
GOD!

Joseph's Well

Lesson Supplies

-Bible Blast Story Card
-kid sock
-pennies
-small garbage can
-Q-tips®
-play food

-It's Okay Days of the Week Poster (from activity pages)

Bible Blast
Joseph's Well

Supplies: *Bible Blast Story Card, kid socks (filled with pennies & tied up)*

Do this: Read the Bible Blast story. Use the kid socks as money bags as you read the Bible Blast story. Don't forget to reinforce the core concept.

Apples to Apples
Thrown Away

Supplies: garbage can, Q-tips®

Do this: Have children take turns tossing the Q-tips® into the garbage can.

Say this: "Remember in our Bible story today – how Joseph's brothers threw him in the well like trash? He could have stayed really mad at them right? Did Joseph stay mad?..."

So Hungry

Supplies: play food items

Do this: Scatter the food around the room. Direct the children to help you gather the food. Recap the Bible story.

Say this: "Do you remember how there wasn't any food in Egypt? And how Joseph helped his brothers because they were so hungry?..."

Bible Bites
Everyday Forgiver

Supplies: It's Okay Days of The Week Poster

Do this: Use the It's Okay Days of The Week Poster as you sing the *It's Okay* chant.

Say this:
*It's okay!
I forgive on Sunday, Monday, Tuesday
It's okay!
I forgive on Wednesday, Thursday, Friday
It's okay!
I forgive on Saturday
I forgive every day!
That's the Jesus way!*

Bye-Bye Bible Review
Love Down Low

Do this: Gather children in a group. At the teacher's cue, have your preschoolers reach up really high, and then reach down really low.

Say this: "God wants us to forgive like Jesus forgives. Do you remember what happened to Joseph in our Bible story today? He was down really, REALLY low! But he still loved and forgave his brothers. He loved down low! Let me see you love down low! Now love up high! Great job!"

Let's Talk Apples!

How amazing it is to learn that we can be just like Jesus! In this lesson series, your 2 & 3 year old toddler friends will have an opportunity to discover how they can Forgive Like Jesus!

Transition Song

I forgive, I forgive
I forgive like JESUS!

Core Concept
I can forgive like Jesus.

I forgive, I forgive
I forgive like JESUS!

Scripture Seed

Forgive each other, just as God forgave you because of what Christ has done.
-Ephesians 4:32 (NIrV)

I forgive, I forgive
I forgive like JESUS!

I forgive, I forgive
I forgive like JESUS!

I forgive just like you
GOD!

Sneaky Stew

Lesson Supplies

-Bible Blast Story Card
-Expression Face Cards (from activity pages)
-pot
-heart cut-outs (from activity pages)
-It's Okay Days of the Week Poster (from activity pages)

Bible Blast
Sneaky Stew

Supplies: *Bible Blast Story Card, mad, scared, & happy face cards*

Do this: Read the Bible Blast story. Use the facial expression cards as you read the Bible Blast story. Don't forget to reinforce the core concept.

Apples to Apples
Love Stew

Supplies: pot, heart cut-outs

Do this: Place the pot in the middle of the floor (or in the middle of the table). Scatter the hearts around the room. Have the children help you make *Love Stew* by putting all the hearts inside the pot. Recap the Bible story.

Say this: *"I'd like to make some Love Stew. Does anyone want to help me? Great! The only thing I need is some love and forgiveness. Can you help me put all the hearts in the pot? In our Bible story today, remember how Jacob tricked his brother with soup? Esau was really mad. Did he stay mad at Jacob?..."*

Very Hairy

Do this: Ask children what kinds of animals have fur. Call out various animals that are hairy. Have children pretend to be those animals.

Say this: *"Remember how Jacob's mommy put goat hair on his arms? That's because Esau's arms were very hairy. What other kinds of animals are hairy? How about sheep? Let's pretend to be sheep!"* (bears, lions, dogs, cats, etc.)

Bible Bites
Everyday Forgiver

Supplies: *It's Okay Days of The Week Poster*

Do this: Use the It's Okay Days of The Week Poster as you sing the *It's Okay* chant.

Say this:
It's okay!
I forgive on Sunday, Monday, Tuesday
It's okay!
I forgive on Wednesday, Thursday, Friday
It's okay!
I forgive on Saturday
I forgive every day!
That's the Jesus way!

Bye-Bye Bible Review
Jump and Shake!

Do this: Gather children in a group and sing the Jump and Shake chant.

Say this:
JUMP! And SHAKE!
That frown away (point to mouth with both hands)
JUMP! And SHAKE!
That frown away (point to mouth with both hands)
JUMP! And SHAKE!
That frown away (point to mouth with both hands)
JUMP and SHAKE and LOVE today!

Let's Talk Apples!

How amazing it is to learn that we can be just like Jesus! In this lesson series, your 2 & 3 year old toddler friends will have an opportunity to discover how they can Forgive Like Jesus!

Core Concept
I can forgive like Jesus.

Scripture Seed

Forgive each other, just as God forgave you because of what Christ has done.
-*Ephesians 4:32 (NIrV)*

Transition Song

I forgive, I forgive
I forgive like JESUS!

I forgive, I forgive
I forgive like JESUS!

I forgive, I forgive
I forgive like JESUS!

I forgive just like you
GOD!

A Very Sorry Son

Lesson Supplies

-Bible Blast Story Card
-two empty toilet tissue rolls
(stapled together to be used as binoculars.)
-play money
-basket

-large heart cut-outs (from activity pages)
-It's Okay Days of the Week Poster (from activity pages)
-Empty paper towel roll (look-through tube)

Bible Blast
A Very Sorry Son

Supplies: *Bible Blast Story Card, binoculars (empty toilet tissue rolls)*

Do this: Read the Bible Blast story. Use the binoculars as you read the Bible Blast story. Don't forget to reinforce the core concept.

Apples to Apples
Lost and Found

Supplies: *play money, basket*

Do this: Scatter play money around the room. Have children help you find your lost money and put it in the basket.

Say this: *"Oh no! I've lost all my money! Can you help me find all my money?"*

I See You!

Supplies: *look-through tube*

Do this: Gather children on the floor or at the table. Use the look-through tube to look at each child while you sing the chant. Do various motions and ask children what they see you doing. Recap the Bible story.

Say this:
(child's name!)
I see you, do you see me?
Tell me what you see!
Repeat with each child.

Bible Bites
Everyday Forgiver

Supplies: *It's Okay Days of The Week Poster*

Do this: Use the It's Okay Days of The Week Poster as you sing the *It's Okay* chant.

Say this:
It's okay!
I forgive on Sunday, Monday, Tuesday
It's okay!
I forgive on Wednesday, Thursday, Friday
It's okay!
I forgive on Saturday
I forgive every day!
That's the Jesus way!

Bye-Bye Bible Review
Love Races

Supplies: *large heart cut-outs*

Do this: Have children color their hearts. For the Love Race, children should place large hearts on their heads and try to get from one side of the room to the other without the heart falling off.

Say this: *"Great job with your hearts! In our Bible story today, the son was really sorry, and his dad was really happy to see him. He loved his son so much, that he ran to him! We're gonna have a love race! Everyone put your hearts on your heads and let's see who can get to the other wall without their heart falling off! Ready, set, go!"*

Let's Talk Apples!

How amazing it is to learn that we can be just like Jesus! In this lesson series, your 2 & 3 year old toddler friends will have an opportunity to discover how they can Forgive Like Jesus!

Core Concept

I can forgive like Jesus.

Scripture Seed

Forgive each other, just as God forgave you because of what Christ has done.
-Ephesians 4:32 (NIrV)

Transition Song

I forgive, I forgive
I forgive like JESUS!

I forgive, I forgive
I forgive like JESUS!

I forgive, I forgive
I forgive like JESUS!

I forgive just like you
GOD!

A Short & Sorry Man

Lesson Supplies

-Bible Blast Story Card
-ruler or measuring stick
-mean/happy face cards (from activity pages)
-upbeat music
-It's Okay Days of the Week Poster (from activity pages)

Bible Blast
A Short and Sorry Man

Supplies: *Bible Blast Story Card, ruler or measuring stick*

Do this: Read the Bible Blast story. Use the ruler as you read the Bible Blast story. Don't forget to reinforce the core concept.

Apples to Apples
Finger Friends!

Do this: Have fun with your fingers! Have children help you compare the size of your fingers. Recap the Bible story.

Say this: *"Ok friends, let me see you wiggle your fingers! Look at my fingers. Which finger is taller? Yup! You got it! Now which finger is shorter? Great job! In our Bible story today, was Zacchaeus tall or short?..."*

Face Fun

Supplies: *mean and happy face cards*

Do this: Gather children on the floor or at the table. Ask children various questions about the Bible story. When the answer is mean, hold up the mean face card and make a mean face. When the answer is nice, hold up the happy face card and make a happy face.

Say this: *"Was Zacchaeus mean, or nice? After he met Jesus did he want to be mean or nice? Was it mean or nice for Jesus to forgive Zacchaeus? Does Jesus want us to be mean or nice?"*

Bible Bites
Everyday Forgiver

Supplies: *It's Okay Days of The Week Poster*

Do this: Use the It's Okay Days of The Week Poster as you sing the *It's Okay* chant.

Say this:
It's okay!
I forgive on Sunday, Monday, Tuesday
It's okay!
I forgive on Wednesday, Thursday, Friday
It's okay!
I forgive on Saturday
I forgive every day!
That's the Jesus way!

Bye-Bye Bible Review
Tree Freeze

Supplies: *upbeat music*

Do this: Play upbeat music. Periodically stop the music. When the music stops, instruct children to freeze like trees in different positions. Re-start the music and repeat.

Say this: *"Remember how Zacchaeus climbed into the tree to see Jesus? That must have been really high! Let me see all of you stand really tall like a tree! What tall trees you are! Whenever the music stops, I want you all to freeze like a tree!"*

Let's Talk Apples!

Isn't it amazing to know that the Bible teaches us how we can be just like Jesus! This series, your 4 & 5 year olds will enjoy exciting stories, songs, and activities as they learn about how we can forgive like Jesus!

Core Concept
I can forgive like Jesus.

Scripture Seed
Forgive each other, just as God forgave you because of what Christ has done.
-Ephesians 4:32 (NIrV)

Transition Song

I forgive, I forgive,
I forgive like JESUS!

I forgive, I forgive,
I forgive like JESUS!

I forgive, I forgive,
I forgive like JESUS!

I forgive just like you GOD!

Joseph's Well

Lesson Supplies

-Bible Blast Story Card
-large laminated tree
-toy apple
-Q-tips®
-garbage can
-kid socks

-pennies
-shape cut-outs (from activity pages)
-basket
-balloons

Apple-tizer
Thrown Away

Supplies: *Garbage can, Q-tips®*

Do this: Have children take turns tossing the Q-tips® into the garbage can.

Say this: *"Great job tossing those Q-tips® into the trash! In our Bible story today, there was a boy who was tossed into a deep well, like trash. Let's read about it."*

Bible Blast
Joseph's Well

Supplies: *Bible Blast Story Card, kid socks (filled with pennies & tied up)*

Do this: Read the Bible Blast story. Use the kid socks as money bags as you read the Bible Blast story. Don't forget to reinforce the core concept.

Apple Tree Chat

Supplies: *large laminated tree poster, toy apple*

Do this: Hang laminated tree on the wall. Have children sit with you next to the tree. Ask children if there is anything that they would like to share about something exciting that happened or is happening in their lives. Only the child with the apple is allowed to share.

Apples to Apples
Crazy Color Dance

Supplies: *balloons (different colors)*

Do this: Pass out different color balloons. Have children sit down on the floor. Call out various colors. Have the children holding the color you call out do a crazy color dance.

Say this: *"Ok are you ready to dance?! Let me see your crazy red dance…I'm just crazy about the color red! If you have a blue balloon let's see your crazy blue dance!…Awesome dancing! Joseph had a coat that had many different colors like the ones we just danced about…"*

Bible Bites
Shaped Like Jesus

Supplies: *laminated shape cut-outs, basket*

Do this: Have children help you name the shapes with the characteristics of Jesus. Talk about each shape and how we can be like Jesus. Ask children to give you examples.

Core Concept Review
Mirror Me!

Do this: Have children mirror your various movements. Allow children to take turns leading while the other children are the mirror. Review the core concept.

Life Lesson I should forgive because God forgives me.

Let's Talk Apples!

Isn't it amazing to know that the Bible teaches us how we can be just like Jesus! This series, your 4 & 5 year olds will enjoy exciting stories, songs, and activities as they learn about how we can forgive like Jesus!

Core Concept
I can forgive like Jesus.

Scripture Seed
Forgive each other, just as God forgave you because of what Christ has done.
-Ephesians 4:32 (NIrV)

Transition Song

I forgive, I forgive,
I forgive like JESUS!

I forgive, I forgive,
I forgive like JESUS!

I forgive, I forgive,
I forgive like JESUS!

I forgive just like you GOD!

Sneaky Stew

Lesson Supplies

-Bible Blast Story Card
-large laminated tree
-toy apple
-big pot or box
-big spoon
-small ballons

-expression face cards (from activity pages)
-shape cut-outs (from activity pages)
-basket

Apple-tizer
Love Soup

Supplies: big pot, big spoon, small balloons

Do this: Blow up small balloons. Have children help you get all the balloons into the pot to make the love soup.

Say this: "Awesome job making that delicious love soup! Have you ever had sneaky soup? We are going to read about some sneaky soup in our Bible Blast story today…"

Bible Blast
Sneaky Stew

Supplies: Bible Blast Story Card, mad, scared, & happy face cards

Do this: Read the Bible Blast story. Use the facial expression cards as you read the Bible Blast story. Don't forget to reinforce the core concept.

Apple Tree Chat

Supplies: large laminated tree poster, toy apple

Do this: Hang laminated tree on the wall. Have children sit with you next to the tree. Ask children if there is anything that they would like to share about something exciting that happened or is happening in their lives. Only the child with the apple is allowed to share.

Apples to Apples
Do You See What I See?

Do this: Describe different objects that you see in the room and have children try to guess what you see. Review the Bible story.

Say this: "Wow, do you all see everything! Remember in our Bible story how Isaac couldn't see? Do you remember what happened?…"

Bible Bites
Shaped Like Jesus

Supplies: *laminated shape cut-outs, basket*

Do this: Have children help you name the shapes with the characteristics of Jesus. Talk about each shape and how we can be like Jesus. Ask children to give you examples.

Core Concept Review
Jump for Joy!

Do this: Sing the Jump for Joy chant. Review the core concept and the life lesson.

Say this:

I'm gonna jump, jump for joy (jump twice)
Because God forgives me
I'm gonna jump, jump for joy (jump twice)
Because God forgives me
I'm gonna jump, jump for joy (jump twice)
Because God forgives me
I forgive you (point at a friend)
Because He forgave me! (point to yourself)

Life Lesson | I should forgive because God forgives me.

Let's Talk Apples!

Isn't it amazing to know that the Bible teaches us how we can be just like Jesus! This series, your 4 & 5 year olds will enjoy exciting stories, songs, and activities as they learn about how we can forgive like Jesus!

Core Concept
I can forgive like Jesus.

Scripture Seed
Forgive each other, just as God forgave you because of what Christ has done.
-*Ephesians 4:32 (NIrV)*

Transition Song

I forgive, I forgive,
I forgive like JESUS!

I forgive, I forgive,
I forgive like JESUS!

I forgive, I forgive,
I forgive like JESUS!

I forgive just like you
GOD!

A Very Sorry Son

Lesson Supplies

-Bible Blast Story Card
-large laminated tree
-toy apple
-empty pickle jar
-pennies
-2 empty toilet tissue rolls (stapled together

for binoculars)
-large heart cut-outs (from activity pages)
-shape cut-outs (from activity pages)
-basket

Apple-tizer
Penny Pickle

Supplies: empty pickle jar, pennies

Do this: Scatter pennies around the room. Have children help you get all the pennies back into the pickle jar.

Say this: "Wow! Everyone did a great job getting all the lost money back. You know, in our Bible Blast story today, there is a young guy who lost all his money too…"

Bible Blast
A Very Sorry Son

Supplies: Bible Blast Story Card, 2 empty toilet paper rolls (to be used as binoculars)

Do this: Read the Bible Blast story. Use the toilet paper rolls as directed in the Bible Blast story. Don't forget to reinforce the core concept.

Apple Tree Chat

Supplies: large laminated tree poster, toy apple

Do this: Hang laminated tree on the wall. Have children sit with you next to the tree. Ask children if there is anything that they would like to share about something exciting that happened or is happening in their lives. Only the child with the apple is allowed to share.

Apples to Apples
Love Races

Supplies: large heart cut-outs

Do this: Have children decorate their hearts. For the Love Race, children should place large hearts on their heads and try to get from one side of the room to the other without the heart falling off.

Say this: "Great job with your hearts! In our Bible story today, the son was really sorry, and his dad was really happy to see him. He loved his son so much, that he ran to him! We're gonna have a love race! Everyone put your hearts on your heads and let's see who can get to the other wall without their heart falling off! Ready, set, go!"

Bible Bites
Shaped Like Jesus

Supplies: *laminated shape cut-outs, basket*

Do this: Have children help you name the shapes with the characteristics of Jesus. Talk about each shape and how we can be like Jesus. Ask children to give you examples.

Core Concept Review
Heart Shout

Do this: Sing the Heart Shout chant. Review the core concept and the life lesson.

Say this:

> *With our mouths we say (point to mouth)*
> *I'm sorry, I forgive you*
> *With our hearts we shout*
> *We wanna be like Jesus! (shout)*
> *With our mouths we say (point to mouth)*
> *I'm sorry, I forgive you*
> *With our hearts we shout*
> *We wanna be like Jesus! (shout)*

Life Lesson I should forgive because God forgives me.

Let's Talk Apples!

Isn't it amazing to know that the Bible teaches us how we can be just like Jesus! This series, your 4 & 5 year olds will enjoy exciting stories, songs, and activities as they learn about how we can forgive like Jesus!

Core Concept
I can forgive like Jesus.

Scripture Seed
Forgive each other, just as God forgave you because of what Christ has done.
-Ephesians 4:32 (NIrV)

Transition Song

I forgive, I forgive,
I forgive like JESUS!

I forgive, I forgive,
I forgive like JESUS!

I forgive, I forgive,
I forgive like JESUS!

I forgive just like you GOD!

A Short & Sorry Man

Lesson Supplies

-Bible Blast Story Card
-large laminated tree
-toy apple
-ruler or measuring stick
-upbeat music

-shape cut-outs (from activity pages)
-basket

Apple-tizer
On Your Knees, Get Set, Go!

Do this: Have children get down on their hands and knees and race from one end of the room to the other.

Say this: *"Whoo hoo! You are all so fast! Did you see how short we all were when we got down on our knees? Today, we are going to read a story about a man who was really short and really sorry..."*

Bible Blast
A Short and Sorry Man

Supplies: *Bible Blast Story Card, ruler or measuring stick*

Do this: Read the Bible Blast story. Use the ruler as instructed in the Bible Blast story. Don't forget to reinforce the core concept.

Apple Tree Chat

Supplies: *large laminated tree poster, toy apple*

Do this: Hang laminated tree on the wall. Have children sit with you next to the tree. Ask children if there is anything that they would like to share about something exciting that happened or is happening in their lives. Only the child with the apple is allowed to share.

Apples to Apples
Tree Freeze

Supplies: *upbeat music*

Do this: Play upbeat music. Periodically stop the music. When the music stops, instruct children to freeze like trees in different positions. Re-start the music and repeat.

Say this: *"Remember how Zacchaeus climbed into the tree to see Jesus? That must have been really high! Let me see all of you stand really tall like a tree! What tall trees you are! Whenever the music stops, I want you all to freeze like a tree!"*

Bible Bites
Shaped Like Jesus

Supplies: *laminated shape cut-outs, basket*

Do this: Have children help you name the shapes with the characteristics of Jesus. Talk about each shape and how we can be like Jesus. Ask children to give you examples.

Core Concept Review
Feast of Forgiveness

Do this: Gather children together in a circle on the floor. Have children take turns saying what their favorite food is. Recap the Bible Blast story. Review the life lesson.

Life Lesson | I should forgive because God forgives me.

Let's Talk Apples!

Speak love and obedience over your babies.

Core Concept
I can obey like Jesus.

Scripture Seed
Anyone who has my commands
and obeys them loves me.
- *John 14:21 (NIrV)*

Transition Song

I wanna be, I wanna be, I wanna be like JESUS!

I wanna be, I wanna be, I wanna be like JESUS!

I wanna be, I wanna be, I wanna be like JESUS!

I wanna be just like you GOD!

Sing the following chant with your babies during diaper changes, feedings, and play time:

When we, we, we
Obey-bey-bey
This is what our hearts say, say
We love, love, love You Jesus
We love when we obey!

Let's Talk Apples!

In this lesson, spend some time teaching your toddlers how we love Jesus when we are obedient.

Core Concept
I can obey like Jesus.

Scripture Seed

Anyone who has my commands and obeys them loves me.
– John 14:21(NIrV)

Transition Song

I wanna be,
I wanna be, I wanna
be like Jesus!

I wanna be,
I wanna be, I wanna
be like Jesus!

I wanna be,
I wanna be, I wanna
be like Jesus!

I wanna be just like
you GOD!

Lesson Supplies

-CD of animal sounds (can choose to download from soundbible.com or another website)
-toddler praise and worship music

Bible Blast
Monkey Do!

Do this: Gather children close to you in an open area in the room. Pretend to be monkeys and have the children do various actions that monkeys might do.

Say this: *"Did you know that monkeys are very good at doing what they see others do? Let's pretend we are monkeys. Follow me! Great job! Jesus wants us to do what he does!"*

Apples to Apples
Up High!

Do this: Have children stand up in an open area. Instruct children to stretch up really high, and then to scrunch down really low. See how fast the children can listen to your directions.

Say this: *"Stretch up really high! Now scrunch down really low. (whisper) Wow, that was fast! None of you were too slow!"*

March With Me

Supplies: *praise and worship music*

Do this: Put on praise and worship music. Lead the children on a march around the room. Periodically, stop the music and shout FREEZE! Restart the music and repeat while children are engaged.

Say this: *"Come march with me! FREEZE! Great job freezing! You were all obedient like Jesus was obedient!"*

Bible Bites
Did You Hear That?

Supplies: *CD of animal sounds*

Do this: Sit children at the table or on the floor in a circle for snack time. Play the CD of animal sounds. Have children help you identify the animals.

Say this: *"Do you know where your ears are? Show me your ears. Great job! God gave us ears so we could listen and obey. We can hear all kinds of things with our ears. Let's listen now and see if we can guess what kinds of animals we hear!"*

Bye-Bye Baby
Follow Me

Do this: Gather children to an open area of the room. Sing the chant while completing the actions. Have children complete actions with you as you sing.

Say this:

> *Touch your ears*
> *Touch your nose*
> *Touch your head*
> *Touch your toes!*
> *Follow me and we will see*
> *How obedient you can be!*

Let's Talk Apples!

How wonderful it has been to discover all the ways that we can be just like Jesus! This series of lessons will teach your 2 & 3 year old friends about how they can obey like Jesus!

Core Concept
I can obey like Jesus.

Scripture Seed

Anyone who has my commands and obeys them loves me.
-John 14:21(NIrV)

Transition Song

I wanna be, I wanna be, I wanna be like JESUS!

I wanna be, I wanna be, I wanna be like JESUS!

I wanna be, I wanna be, I wanna be like JESUS!

I wanna be just like you GOD!

A Big Fish

Lesson Supplies

-Bible Blast Story Card
-fish stickers
-spray bottle
-small water balloons

-large plastic bowl
-bubbles

Bible Blast
A Big Fish

Supplies: *Bible Blast Story Card, fish stickers, spray bottle*

Do this: Read the Bible Blast story. Place a fish sticker on each child's hand. Use the spray bottle as you read the Bible story. Don't forget to reinforce the core concept.

Apples to Apples
Go Fish!

Supplies: *small water balloons, large plastic bowl*

Do this: Scatter the water balloons around the room and have the children help you get them back into the bowl. Recap the Bible story.

Say this: *"There are an awful lot of fish out here in the sea. Let's be fishers! Can you help me catch all these fish and put them in the bowl?"*

Fish Follow

Do this: Gather children together. Pretend to be a fish. Instruct children to follow everything that you do as a fish. (Make fish lips, swim like a fish, jump out of the water, eat, etc.)

Say this: *"We're going to pretend to be fish. Let's see how well you can follow me fish!"*

Bible Bites
Bubble Obey

Supplies: *Bubbles*

Do this: Blow bubbles while you sing the *Bubble Obey* chant.

Say this:
> *I bubble obey,*
> *Bubble obey*
> *I do whatever Jesus says without a delay*
> *I bubble, bubble, bubble, obey!*

*Repeat using mom, dad, teacher, etc.

Bye-Bye Bible Review
God Said Go!

Do this: Recap the Bible story. Call out various motions to have the children follow.

Say this: *"God told Jonah to GO! But Jonah wasn't obedient. We should always be obedient to God. Let's practice being obedient. God says jump... crawl... turn around... put your hands up... etc.)"*

Let's Talk Apples!

How wonderful it has been to discover all the ways that we can be just like Jesus! This series of lessons will teach your 2 & 3 year old friends about how they can obey like Jesus!

Core Concept
I can obey like Jesus.

Scripture Seed

Anyone who has my commands and obeys them loves me.
-John 14:21(NIrV)

Transition Song

I wanna be, I wanna be, I wanna be like JESUS!

I wanna be, I wanna be, I wanna be like JESUS!

I wanna be, I wanna be, I wanna be like JESUS!

I wanna be just like you GOD!

Good Sheep

Lesson Supplies

-Bible Blast Story Card
-cotton balls
-basket
-bubbles
-whistle

Bible Blast
Good Sheep

Supplies: *Bible Blast Story Card, whistle*

Do this: Read the Bible Blast story. Use the whistle as directed in the Bible story. Don't forget to reinforce the core concept.

Apples to Apples
Sheep Shake

Do this: Have children pretend to be sheep. Call out various body parts and have children shake them.

Say this: *"Ok, let's see how well all my little sheep listen! Sheep shake your arms! Sheep shake your feet! Sheep shake your head! Wow, you all are such great shakers!"*

Follow the Shepherd

Do this: Gather children together. Move around the room doing various actions. Have children follow you and do what you do.

Say this: *"Ok friends, I want you to follow everything that I do. I am going to pretend that I am the shepherd from our story today. Are you ready?"*

Bible Bites
Bubble Obey

Supplies: Bubbles

Do this: Blow bubbles while you sing the *Bubble Obey* chant.

Say this:
> I bubble obey,
> Bubble obey
> I do whatever Jesus says without a delay
> I bubble, bubble, bubble, obey!

*Repeat using mom, dad, teacher, etc.

Bye-Bye Bible Review
Scared Sheep

Supplies: cotton balls, basket

Do this: Scatter the cotton balls all around the room. Have the children help you return the cotton balls (sheep) to the basket (sheep pen). Recap the Bible story.

Say this: *"Oh no! The sheep are scared of the wolves and they've all run away. Can you help me get them back into the pen?"*

Let's Talk Apples!

How wonderful it has been to discover all the ways that we can be just like Jesus! This series of lessons will teach your 2 & 3 year old friends about how they can obey like Jesus!

Core Concept
I can obey like Jesus.

Scripture Seed

Anyone who has my commands and obeys them loves me.
-John 14:21(NIrV)

Transition Song

I wanna be, I wanna be, I wanna be like JESUS!

I wanna be, I wanna be, I wanna be like JESUS!

I wanna be, I wanna be, I wanna be like JESUS!

I wanna be just like you GOD!

A Big Boat

Lesson Supplies

-Bible Blast Story Card
-large Legos®
-spray bottle
-handheld mirror

-hula hoops
-upbeat music
-bubbles

Bible Blast
A Big Boat

Supplies: *Bible Blast Story Card, large Legos®, spray bottle*

Do this: Read the Bible Blast story. Hand each child a Lego® and have them stack them on top of each other while you read the Bible story. Use the spray bottle as directed in the Bible story. Don't forget to reinforce the core concept.

Apples to Apples
Two Times!

Do this: Ask children to do various movements twice. Review the Bible story.

Say this: "Can you jump two times? Great job! Now, clap two times.... stomp two times... How many of each animal did God tell Noah to bring on the boat?..."

Who is That?

Supplies: hand held mirror

Do this: Sit children at the table. Allow each child to see themselves in the mirror and ask them their names.

Say this: "Can you see yourselves? What is your name? (child's name) obeys like Jesus!"

Bible Bites
Bubble Obey

Supplies: Bubbles

Do this: Blow bubbles while you sing the *Bubble Obey* chant.

Say this:

I bubble obey,
Bubble obey
I do whatever Jesus says without a delay
I bubble, bubble, bubble, obey!

*Repeat using mom, dad, teacher, etc.

Bye-Bye Bible Review
Into the Boat

Supplies: hula hoops, spray bottles, upbeat music

Do this: Play upbeat music and place hula hoops in various places around the room. Stop the music periodically and direct children to jump inside the hula hoops. Lightly spray children not standing in the hula hoops with the spray bottle. (spray water upward so that it falls on the children, rather than spraying them directly)

Say this: "Ok, I want to see how quickly you can get into the boat before the rain comes. We are going to pretend that these hula hoops are boats – just like the one that God told Noah to build. When the music stops, I want everyone to stand inside of a hula hoop. If you're not inside of the hula hoop, the rain is going to get you all wet. Are you ready?!"

Let's Talk Apples!

How wonderful it has been to discover all the ways that we can be just like Jesus! This series of lessons will teach your 2 & 3 year old friends about how they can obey like Jesus!

Core Concept
I can obey like Jesus.

Scripture Seed

Anyone who has my commands and obeys them loves me.
-John 14:21(NIrV)

Transition Song

I wanna be, I wanna be, I wanna be like JESUS!

I wanna be, I wanna be, I wanna be like JESUS!

I wanna be, I wanna be, I wanna be like JESUS!

I wanna be just like you GOD!

Tree Trouble

Lesson Supplies

-Bible Blast Story Card
-play fruit
-fruit cards (from activity pages)
-bubbles

Bible Blast
Tree Trouble

Supplies: *Bible Blast Story Card, play fruit*

Do this: Read the Bible Blast story. Hand each child a piece of pretend fruit. Keep one piece for the story teller to use as directed in the Bible story. Don't forget to reinforce the core concept.

Apples to Apples
Rainbow Fruit

Supplies: *play fruit*

Do this: Ask children to help you name all the colors of the fruit.

Say this: "Does anyone like fruit? I love fruit! Fruit can be many colors. Let's see if we can name all the colors of this fruit. Can you help me?"

Right & Left

Do this: Have children follow you as you hold out your right arm and move to the right. Then hold out your left arm and move to the left. Recap the Bible story.

Say this: "We are going to play Right & Left to see how well you all listen. It's just like in our Bible story today. Adam and Eve didn't obey God. We are going to see how well you can obey. When I say go right, I want you to move to the right. When I say left, I want you to move to the left. Got it?"

Bible Bites
Bubble Obey

Supplies: *Bubbles*

Do this: Blow bubbles while you sing the *Bubble Obey* chant.

Say this:

> I bubble obey,
> Bubble obey
> I do whatever Jesus says without a delay
> I bubble, bubble, bubble, obey!

*Repeat using mom, dad, teacher, etc.

Bye-Bye Bible Review
Happy Fruit

Supplies: *fruit cards activity page*

Do this: Review the Bible story. As you review, ask children about whether God was happy or sad. Hold up a fruit card when the answer is happy.

Say this: "Do you remember in our Bible story today how God made Adam and Eve? Was God happy or sad that he made Adam and Eve? He was very happy! Here's a happy fruit. What is this? When Adam and Eve ate the fruit that God told them not to eat, was God happy or sad? He was very sad because they didn't obey. Is God happy or sad when we obey? He's happy..."

Let's Talk Apples!

How wonderful it has been to discover all the ways that we can be just like Jesus! This series of lessons will teach your 2 & 3 year old friends about how they can obey like Jesus!

Core Concept
I can obey like Jesus.

Scripture Seed

Anyone who has my commands and obeys them loves me.
-John 14:21(NIrV)

Transition Song

I wanna be, I wanna be, I wanna be like JESUS!

I wanna be, I wanna be, I wanna be like JESUS!

I wanna be, I wanna be, I wanna be like JESUS!

I wanna be just like you GOD!

Follow Me

Lesson Supplies

-Bible Blast Story Card
-stick
-yarn
-paper clip
-blue construction paper (or blue poster board)
-tape
-bubbles

Bible Blast
Follow Me

Supplies: *Bible Blast Story Card, fishing pole (make a fishing pole with a stick, yarn, and paper clip)*

Do this: Read the Bible Blast story. Use the fishing pole as directed in the Bible story. Don't forget to reinforce the core concept.

Apples to Apples
Puddle Pounce

Supplies: *puddle cut-outs (make puddles out of blue construction paper or blue poster board)*

Do this: Tape puddle cut-outs to the floor. Have children follow you as you pounce from one puddle to the next.

Say this: *"Does anyone like to splash in puddles? Well, let's pretend to splash in these puddles. Can you follow me the way that Jesus' friends followed him?"*

Calling All Children!

Do this: Sit in an area of the classroom and call each child by name to come over to you. Tell each child that they did a great job listening and that you are so happy that they are obedient just like Jesus.

Say this: *"Child's name! Wow, you are such a great listener! I'm so glad that you are obedient just like Jesus!"*

Bible Bites
Bubble Obey

Supplies: Bubbles

Do this: Blow bubbles while you sing the *Bubble Obey* chant.

Say this:
> *I bubble obey,*
> *Bubble obey*
> *I do whatever Jesus says without a delay*
> *I bubble, bubble, bubble, obey!*

*Repeat using mom, dad, teacher, etc.

Bye-Bye Bible Review
Can You Hear Me Now?

Do this: This is a listening activity. Gather children to the center of the room. Whisper various gestures and see how well children can follow your lead.

Say this: *"Let's play a listening game. I'm going to make my voice really quiet so you will have to be very quiet to hear me. Ready? If you can hear me... touch your toes... If you can hear me... touch your eyes... touch your nose... raise your hands... etc. Awesome job listening everyone!"*

Let's Talk Apples!

In this final lesson series, your preschoolers will begin to understand how important it is to be obedient. Through songs, games and structured activities, children will discover that they can be obedient like Jesus!

Core Concept
I can obey like Jesus.

Scripture Seed
Anyone who has my commands and obeys them loves me.
-John 14:21(NIrV)

Transition Song

I wanna be, I wanna be, I wanna be like JESUS!

I wanna be, I wanna be, I wanna be like JESUS!

I wanna be, I wanna be, I wanna be like JESUS!

I wanna be just like you GOD!

A Big Fish
Lesson Supplies

-Bible Blast Story Card
-large laminated tree
-toy apple
-stoplight pages (from activity pages)
-fish stickers

-red, yellow, green, blue paper
-spray bottle
-house activity page (from activity pages)

Apple-tizer
Stop and Go!

Supplies: *stoplight activity page*

Do this: Have children try to get from one side of the room to the other. They can only move when the green GO card is raised up. Switch between the green and red cards.

Say this: *"You all did an excellent job obeying the traffic lights! In our Bible story today, we are going to read about a man who didn't go when God told him to…"*

Bible Blast
A Big Fish

Supplies: *Bible Blast Story Card, spray bottle, fish stickers*

Do this: Before you read the Bible Blast story, place a fish sticker on each child's hand. Use the spray bottle as you read the Bible story. Every time you say the word fish in the story, have children make fish lips. Don't forget to reinforce the core concept.

Apple Tree Chat

Supplies: *large laminated tree poster, toy apple*

Do this: Hang laminated tree on the wall. Have children sit with you next to the tree. Ask children if there is anything that they would like to share about something exciting that happened or is happening in their lives. Only the child with the apple is allowed to share.

Apples to Apples
Color Corners

Supplies: *red, yellow, green, & blue paper*

Do this: Tape one sheet of color paper in each corner. Call out different colors. Whatever color you call out, have children rush to that corner. Recap the Life Lesson.

Bible Bites
Me and My House

Supplies: *House activity page*

Do this: Go through the windows on the House activity page and ask children the questions in the windows. Recap the scripture seed and the life lesson.

Core Concept Review
God Said Go!

Do this: Recap the Bible story. Call out various motions to have the children follow. Review the life lesson.

Say this: *"God told Jonah to GO! But Jonah wasn't obedient. We should always be obedient to God. Let's practice being obedient. God says jump... crawl... turn around... put your hands up... etc.)"*

Life Lesson   I can listen and obey!

Let's Talk Apples!

In this final lesson series, your preschoolers will begin to understand how important it is to be obedient. Through songs, games and structured activities, children will discover that they can be obedient like Jesus!

Core Concept
I can obey like Jesus.

Scripture Seed
Anyone who has my commands and obeys them loves me.
-John 14:21(NIrV)

Transition Song

I wanna be, I wanna be, I wanna be like JESUS!

I wanna be, I wanna be, I wanna be like JESUS!

I wanna be, I wanna be, I wanna be like JESUS!

I wanna be just like you GOD!

Good Sheep

Lesson Supplies

-Bible Blast Story Card
-large laminated tree
-toy apple
-whistle

-house activity page
(from activity pages)

Apple-tizer
Follow the Shepherd

Supplies: whistle

Do this: Gather children together. Move around the room doing various actions. Blow the whistle to have children stop. Then blow the whistle again to have children begin to follow you and do what you do.

Say this: *"Great job following everything that I did! In our Bible Blast story today, we are going to learn about the Good Shepherd..."*

Bible Blast
Good Sheep

Supplies: Bible Blast Story Card, whistle

Do this: Read the Bible Blast story. Use the whistle when you are directed to do so in the story. Don't forget to reinforce the core concept.

Apple Tree Chat

Supplies: large laminated tree poster, toy apple

Do this: Hang laminated tree on the wall. Have children sit with you next to the tree. Ask children if there is anything that they would like to share about something exciting that happened or is happening in their lives. Only the child with the apple is allowed to share.

Apples to Apples
Sheep Shake

Do this: Have children pretend to be sheep. Call out various body parts and have children shake them.

Say this: *"Ok, let's see how well all my little sheep listen! Sheep shake your arms! Sheep shake your feet! Sheep shake your head! Wow, you all are such great shakers!"*

Supplies: *House activity page*

Do this: Go through the windows on the House activity page and ask children the questions in the windows. Recap the scripture seed and the life lesson.

Life Lesson Review
Say What?

Do this: Sit in a circle with the children. Make sure that teachers are at the beginning and end of the circle. The teacher should start first by whispering the life lesson into the ear of the child sitting next to them. That child will then whisper into their neighbor's ear what was whispered into their ear, and so forth. The teacher at the end of the circle should say aloud what was whispered in their ear. Review the life lesson. Repeat with other fun phrases/words from the Bible lesson.

Life Lesson   I can listen and obey!

Let's Talk Apples!

In this final lesson series, your preschoolers will begin to understand how important it is to be obedient. Through songs, games and structured activities, children will discover that they can be obedient like Jesus!

Core Concept
I can obey like Jesus.

Scripture Seed
Anyone who has my commands and obeys them loves me.
-John 14:21(NIrV)

Transition Song

I wanna be, I wanna be, I wanna be like JESUS!

I wanna be, I wanna be, I wanna be like JESUS!

I wanna be, I wanna be, I wanna be like JESUS!

I wanna be just like you GOD!

A Big Boat

Lesson Supplies

-Bible Blast Story Card
-large laminated tree
-toy apple
-white butcher paper
-crayons
-spray bottle
-Legos®

-sticker search activity
 (from activity pages)
-animal stickers
-house activity
 (from activity pages)
-inflatable beach ball

Apple-tizer
Favorite Animals

Supplies: *butcher paper, crayons*

Do this: Cut a long sheet of butcher paper. Either tape it to the wall at children's height or place it on a hard surface. Have children draw their favorite animals on the paper. Go through each of the animals and find out what each child's favorite animal is.

Say this: *"Wow! Look at all these animals. In our Bible Blast story today, we are going read about how God told Noah to do something very important for all these animals…"*

Bible Blast
A Big Boat

Supplies: *Bible Blast Story Card, spray bottle, Legos®*

Do this: Read the Bible Blast story. Use the spray bottle and Legos® as directed in the Bible story. Don't forget to reinforce the core concept.

Apple Tree Chat

Supplies: *large laminated tree poster, toy apple*

Do this: Hang laminated tree on the wall. Have children sit with you next to the tree. Ask children if there is anything that they would like to share about something exciting that happened or is happening in their lives. Only the child with the apple is allowed to share.

Apples to Apples
Sticker Search

Supplies: *sticker search activity page, animal stickers*

Do this: Hide the stickers in the room in a location according to the activity map where children would not be able to find them. Use the Sticker Search Activity Map to have the children help you find the lost stickers. Call out the directions so that children can participate. Once you find the stickers, give each child a sticker. Recap the Bible Blast story.

Say this: *"Great job everyone! If we didn't follow these directions exactly, we would have never found these stickers!"*

Supplies: *House activity page*

Do this: Go through the windows on the House activity page and ask children the questions in the windows. Recap the scripture seed and the life lesson.

Supplies: *Inflatable Beach Ball*

Do this: Take turns tossing the beach ball to the children. Whenever the ball hits the floor, choose a child to repeat the life lesson.

Life Lesson I can listen and obey!

Let's Talk Apples!

In this final lesson series, your preschoolers will begin to understand how important it is to be obedient. Through songs, games and structured activities, children will discover that they can be obedient like Jesus!

Transition Song

I wanna be, I wanna be, I wanna be like JESUS!

I wanna be, I wanna be, I wanna be like JESUS!

I wanna be, I wanna be, I wanna be like JESUS!

I wanna be just like you GOD!

Core Concept
I can obey like Jesus.

Scripture Seed
Anyone who has my commands and obeys them loves me.
-John 14:21(NIrV)

Tree Trouble

Lesson Supplies

-Bible Blast Story Card
-large laminated tree
-toy apple
-red, yellow, green balloons
-Legos®
-house activity page (from activity pages)
-alphabet fruit coloring page (from activity pages)

Apple-tizer
Don't Look!

Supplies: red, yellow, green *balloons*

Do this: Blow up 3 balloons. Have children sit with you on the floor. Instruct children to close their eyes. Take out one balloon at a time, but instruct children not to look at them.

Say this: *"I have a really cool red balloon – but I don't want you to look at it. Awe, you looked! I have a really cool yellow balloon, but I don't want you to look at it. You peaked! It's pretty hard not to do something that looks so cool right? That's kind of what happens in our Bible Blast story today..."*

Bible Blast
Tree Trouble

Supplies: *Bible Blast Story Card, alphabet fruit coloring page*

Do this: Before you read the Bible Blast story, pass out alphabet fruit coloring pages and have children color/decorate (to be used in Bible Blast story). Don't forget to reinforce the core concept.

Apple Tree Chat

Supplies: *large laminated tree poster, toy apple*

Do this: Hang laminated tree on the wall. Have children sit with you next to the tree. Ask children if there is anything that they would like to share about something exciting that happened or is happening in their lives. Only the child with the apple is allowed to share.

Apples to Apples
No Red Bricks

Supplies: *Legos®*

Do this: Have children help you build a house without using any red Legos®. Instruct children not to use any red Legos® in their houses. Recap the Bible Blast story and the life lesson.

Supplies: *House activity page*

Do this: Go through the windows on the House activity page and ask children the questions in the windows. Recap the scripture seed and the life lesson.

Do this: Alternate making various sounds with your body. Have children do whatever you do. (ie. clap your hands, stomp your feet, snap your fingers, cluck your tongue, etc.) Review the life lesson.

Life Lesson   I can listen and obey!

Let's Talk Apples!

In this final lesson series, your preschoolers will begin to understand how important it is to be obedient. Through songs, games and structured activities, children will discover that they can be obedient like Jesus!

Core Concept
I can obey like Jesus.

Scripture Seed
Anyone who has my commands and obeys them loves me.
-John 14:21(NIrV)

Transition Song

I wanna be, I wanna be, I wanna be like JESUS!

I wanna be, I wanna be, I wanna be like JESUS!

I wanna be, I wanna be, I wanna be like JESUS!

I wanna be just like you GOD!

Follow Me

Lesson Supplies

-Bible Blast Story Card
-large laminated tree
-toy apple
-stick
-yarn
-paper clip

-sticky labels
-house activity page
(from activity pages)

Apple-tizer
Frozen Fish

Do this: Instruct children to pretend they are fish that have been frozen in a pond. The teacher should pretend to swim around the room and touch the heads of the children to unfreeze them. Once unfrozen, children should follow the teacher around the room swimming to unfreeze the other children.

Say this: *"You were all really frozen fish! I'm so glad I was able to unfreeze you so you could follow me. You know what? That's just like in our Bible Blast story today!"*

Bible Blast
Follow Me

Supplies: *Bible Blast Story Card, fishing pole (make a fishing pole with a stick, yarn, and paper clip)*

Do this: Read the Bible Blast story. Use the fishing pole as directed in the Bible story. Don't forget to reinforce the core concept.

Apple Tree Chat

Supplies: *large laminated tree poster, toy apple*

Do this: Hang laminated tree on the wall. Have children sit with you next to the tree. Ask children if there is anything that they would like to share about something exciting that happened or is happening in their lives. Only the child with the apple is allowed to share.

Apples to Apples
Number Scrunch

Supplies: *labels*

Do this: Write a number from one to four on each label. Give each child one label to stick on their shirts. Call out numbers between one and four. When you call out their number, those children should scrunch down to the floor really low. Review the scripture seed and the life lesson.

Bible Bites
Me and My House

Supplies: *House activity page*

Do this: Go through the windows on the House activity page and ask children the questions in the windows. Recap the scripture seed and the life lesson.

Life Lesson Review
Calling All Children!

Do this: Have children sit on the floor. When you call out various descriptions, those children that have what is being described should stand up/sit down, etc. Recap the life lesson.

Say this: *"If you are wearing blue pants, stand up. If you are wearing earrings stand up.... Great job listening and obeying!"*

BIBLE BLAST
STORY CARDS

Bible Blast

A Very Kind Man
Luke 10

This is a story about a young man who was very kind. Once, there was a man who was traveling along a road going from Jerusalem to Jericho. All of a sudden, some mean robbers beat him up, took all his clothes, and left him lying on the road. Oh no! The man was badly hurt. Soon after, a baker came walking along the same road. (hold up cupcake pan) The baker saw the hurt man lying on the road. He just rushed right by him! "Sorry, he said, but I have cupcakes in the oven and I don't want them to burn!" Then, a mailman passed by the hurt man. (hold up envelopes) Do you think he helped him? **(pause for a response)** No! He did not stop to help. "I don't have time to be kind today," he said. "I still have all these letters to deliver!" Finally, a young man on his way to a baseball game came strolling down the same road. (put on baseball cap) He saw the hurt man. Do you know what? He stopped to help him! He was so kind to the hurt man. He gave him water, and he cleaned up his cuts and bruises. Then, he took him to a safe place where he could rest and he paid someone to take care of him. Wow, he was so kind! He was kind just like Jesus is kind. And we can be kind like Jesus too!

At the core: I can be KIND like Jesus!

Bible Blast

A Very Kind Lady
Luke 21

On a little corner, in a small town, there lived a sweet lady. She was very poor. She didn't have enough money for food, or clothes, or candy, or toys! There was something very special about this lady. Want to know what it was? **(pause)** She was very kind. One day, the townspeople had a festival to raise money for the church. The rich people had lots of money and gave a lot to the church. The kind lady really wanted to give too. The only money that she had was two small coins, just like these. (hold up the pennies) But - do you know what?! She was so kind, and she loved God so much, that she gave the only two coins that she had! Isn't that awesome! And do you know what else? We can be kind and giving too!

At the core: I can be KIND like Jesus!

Bible Blast

Very Kind Friends
Luke 5

Some time ago, there was a man who couldn't walk. He couldn't use his legs to dance, or run, or jump, or anything! It just so happened, that this man had some really kind friends! They knew that Jesus was nearby and they wanted to help their friend who couldn't walk. But, there were so many people around Jesus, that they could hardly see him! (squint your eyes) So, guess what they did? They cut a hole in the roof of the house that Jesus was in! (Show children the plastic cup with the hole in the bottom; put your hand through the cup) Then they lowered their friend through the hole in the roof so that he was right in front of Jesus! Jesus was so pleased with their kindness and their faith, that he healed their friend! Immediately, the man who couldn't walk jumped up and began to dance and thank God! Isn't it wonderful to have kind friends! God wants us to be kind friends too!

At the core: I can be KIND like Jesus!

Bible Blast

A Very Kind King
Matthew 18

There once was a man who lived in a beautiful kingdom that sat high upon a hill. He served the King who was very kind. He loved his people and always treated them kindly. The King's servant borrowed some money from the King and he couldn't pay him back. Actually, he borrowed LOTS of money! (hold up the big dollar) The servant begged the King not to put him in jail. The King was kind, and he felt sorry for his servant. Instead of putting him in jail, he forgave him and told him that he didn't have to pay him back. But then, do you know what the servant did? He saw a man who owed him money….a little bit of money. (hold up the small dollar) Instead of being kind like the King, he was mean and he threw the man in jail! Well, when the King heard about this he was not happy. He couldn't believe that after he was so kind to his servant that he could be so mean to someone else. Right away he called for his servant and told him how disappointed he was with him. He put him in jail until he could pay back the LOTS of money that he owed. (hold up the big dollar) The King wanted his servant to show kindness because he was shown kindness. God wants us to be kind just like Jesus!

At the core: I can be KIND like Jesus!

Bible Blast

Joseph's Well
Genesis 37

Long ago, there was a young boy named Joseph. Joseph had 11 brothers! Count with me! (count to 11) Joseph was the baby of the family. His brothers didn't like him because they thought their dad loved Joseph more than the rest of them. Joseph's dad did love Joseph. He gave him a special coat of many colors to wear. Joseph's brothers were very jealous and so they planned to get rid of Joseph. One day Joseph's father, Jacob, asked him to check on his brothers. When Joseph reached his brothers, they took his coat of colors and through him in a well! Then, they sold him to some traders for eight ounces of silver. (hold up the sock money bag) Joseph was taken to Egypt where he went from being a slave to the governor. He created a plan to keep the people of Egypt from starving during the famine. While Joseph was giving food to the people, he noticed his brothers in the line waiting for food! Joseph was still a little upset about what his brothers did to him. After all, they sold him and separated him from his mom and dad. But Joseph saw how sorry his brothers were and he forgave them. Joseph was so happy to see his family again and they all came to live with him in Egypt. Joseph forgave his brothers and God wants us to forgive each other too!

At the core: I can FORGIVE like Jesus!

Bible Blast

Sneaky Stew
Genesis 25, 27, 33

Jacob and Esau were twin boys. That means that they were born at the same time! But, Esau was born first which meant that he got to get something very special – his father's blessing! Jacob really wanted his father's blessing. His mom wanted him to have it too. One day, Jacob cooked some delicious stew. What do you think was in it? **(pause and allow children to name food items)** Well, Esau came from hunting and he was sooo hungry. Jacob told him that if he gave him their father's blessing, he would give him some stew. Guess what! He did! Then Jacob and his mom tricked his dad into giving him the blessing. Jacob covered himself in goat skins to be hairy like his brother Esau and tricked his poor dad who could hardly see anything! When Esau found out, he was very angry. (hold up the mad face) He was so mad that he chased Jacob and Jacob ran far away. But later, Esau found Jacob. Jacob was so scared. (hold up the scared face) He thought that Esau was still angry with him. But do you know what happened? Esau was so happy to see his brother Jacob! (hold up the happy face card) He ran up to him and gave him a big hug! Esau forgave Jacob just like God wants us to forgive each other!

At the core: I can FORGIVE like Jesus!

Bible Blast

A Very Sorry Son
Luke 15

There was a man who had two sons. How many sons did he have? **(pause to allow children to answer)** Great! He had two sons. The younger son told his dad that he wanted to be on his own. So his father gave him his share of his property and let his son go. Soon after, the younger son wasted all of his money and didn't have anything left! He was very unhappy. He had to work feeding pigs. He was so hungry, that he wished he could eat what the pigs were eating. Finally he realized that life with his father was far better, so he headed home. But listen to this! (Use the paper towel/toilet paper roll binoculars) His father was waiting and watching for him to come home! He thought that his dad would be angry at him but his father loved him so much! He forgave him and cleaned him up. God forgives us the same way. He wants us to forgive each other too!

At the core: I can FORGIVE like Jesus!

Bible Blast

A Short & Sorry Man
Luke 19

This is a story about a short man named Zacchaeus. Zacchaeus was a tax collector who was very short and not very nice. (Use the measuring stick or ruler to measure a few children) He cheated many people out of their money. Zacchaeus desperately wanted to see Jesus. Crowds and crowds of people surrounded Jesus and Zacchaeus was simply too short to see him. So, do you know what he did? Zacchaeus ran ahead and climbed up a tree near where Jesus was going to pass by, just so he could see Jesus! Jesus knew that Zacchaeus was in the tree and made plans to stay at his house. The people heard Jesus and began to murmur. Zacchaeus was not an honest man. They couldn't understand why Jesus would want to stay at the house of a sinner. But once Zacchaeus met Jesus, he wanted to change how he treated people. He promised to give back four times as much as he took from the people. Count with me! (Count to four) Jesus forgave Zacchaeus and he wants us to forgive people too!

At the core: I can FORGIVE like Jesus!

Bible Blast

A Big Fish
Jonah 1-3

This is a story about a man named Jonah. God told Jonah to go to a city called Ninevah. He wanted him to speak to the people about the bad things they were doing. Jonah didn't want to go. He hopped on a boat and sailed to Tarshish. While Jonah and the rest of the crew were at sea, God sent a fierce storm that rocked the boat. (spray the spray bottle into the air) The captain of the boat and the rest of the crew were very scared. But Jonah was sleeping! They woke him up and pleaded with Jonah to ask his God for help, but Jonah knew that the storm was his fault. He was not obedient when God told him to go to Ninevah. He told the men to throw him overboard! They thought he was crazy! But, they threw him overboard! All of a sudden, the sea grew calm. Oh no! What happened to Jonah?! Well, God sent a big fish to come and swallow Jonah so that he would be safe. (instruct children to hold up their hands with their fish stickers) He was inside of the fish's belly for three days and three nights! Then, the fish spit him out onto the dry ground. Jonah decided that he would obey God, and he set off for Ninevah. We should always obey God too!

At the core: I can OBEY like Jesus!

Bible Blast

Good Sheep
John 10

Does anyone know what a shepherd is? **(pause for response)** A shepherd is someone who takes care of sheep, just like God takes care of us. Shepherds love and protect their sheep. Do you know what else? The sheep are obedient only to the shepherd because they know the shepherd's voice. It's like a coach with a whistle. (blow the whistle) When the coach blows the whistle, the players know to listen. Well, the sheep follow the shepherd because they know that the shepherd is good, and they want to be good sheep! We can be good sheep! We can be obedient too!

At the core: I can OBEY like Jesus!

Bible Blast

A Big Boat
Genesis 6

Once there lived a man named Noah who loved and obeyed God. The world was full of people who did very bad things and did not obey God. God told Noah that he was going to flood the earth with water and destroy all the people. (spray the spray bottle in the air) He told Noah to build an ark – a really big boat – for him and his family and to take one male and one female of every animal with them. (stack the Legos®) God was very specific with how Noah was to build the ark and Noah did everything that God told him to do. God saved Noah and his family. Noah was obedient to God and God wants us to be obedient too!

At the core: I can OBEY like Jesus!

Bible Blast

Tree Trouble
Genesis 3

In the beginning, before me, and you, and your mommies, and daddies, there was God. God created the first man and the first woman. He named the man Adam, and the woman Eve. Adam and Eve lived in the Garden of Eden. It was beautiful and they had everything that they needed. God told Adam and Eve that they could eat fruit from any tree that they wanted except for one tree – the tree of the knowledge of good and evil. (have children hold up their fruit) The serpent was in the garden and he tricked Eve. So Eve disobeyed God and ate fruit from the tree that God told her not to. She gave some fruit to Adam and he ate it too. Once they ate the fruit, they realized they were naked, so they made clothes out of fig leaves and they hid from God. But God knew where they were. God was very disappointed with Adam and Eve because they were disobedient. God loved Adam and Eve, so he disciplined them for being disobedient. God loves us very much too, and he wants us to be obedient!

At the core: I can OBEY like Jesus!

Bible Blast

Follow Me
Matthew 4

Jesus was walking along the Sea of Galilee when he saw Peter and Andrew fishing in a boat on the lake. Jesus said, "follow me! I will make you fishers of men!" (dangle the fishing pole) Immediately, Peter and Andrew followed Jesus. Then, Jesus met James and John who were also fishermen. They were fishing with their father. Jesus called out to them and said, "follow me!" (dangle your fishing pole) Immediately, James and John followed Jesus. Peter, Andrew, James, and John followed Jesus. When he called them, they obeyed. We can obey too!

At the core: I can OBEY like Jesus!

PARENT PACTS

Just Like Jesus

Talking Apples!
During this series, spend time talking with your little one about what it means to be kind. Comment on times when you notice that they are being kind and give them extra praise for it. Talk about the importance of being kind, and how they feel when others are kind to them.

This lesson series...
KIND LIKE JESUS

Lesson 1: A Very Kind Man
(Luke 10)

Lesson 2: A Very Kind Lady
(Luke 21)

Lesson 3: Very Kind Friends
(Luke 5)

Lesson 4: A Very Kind King
(Matthew 18)

Core Concept
I can be kind like Jesus.

Scripture Seed
...Always try to be kind to each other and to everyone else.
– 1Thessalonians 5:15 (NIrV)

Life Lesson
I should be kind and help others.

Planting God's Word into children one seed at a time

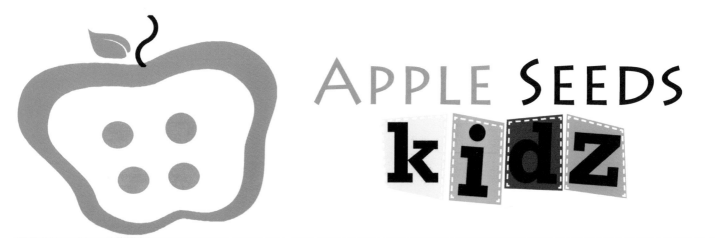

Just Like Jesus

Talking Apples!
Over the next few weeks, help your little ones to connect forgiveness with love. As you notice situations with siblings or friends where forgiveness is required, take some extra time to praise their loving actions.

This lesson series...
FORGIVE LIKE JESUS

Lesson 1: Joseph's Well
(Genesis 37)

Lesson 2: Sneaky Stew
(Genesis 25)

Lesson 3: A Very Sorry Son
(Luke 15)

Lesson 4: A Short & Sorry Man
(Luke 19)

Core Concept
I can forgive like Jesus.

Scripture Seed
Forgive each other, just as God forgave you because of what Christ has done.
– *Ephesians 4:32 (NIrV)*

Life Lesson
I should forgive because God forgives me.

Planting God's Word into children one seed at a time

Just Like Jesus

Talking Apples!
Obedience is a choice, and your little ones are just learning about making choices. Spend some time during this lesson series talking about making good choices. Be sure to show good listening skills so that your toddlers know what you expect from them.

This lesson series...

OBEY LIKE JESUS

Lesson 1: A Big Fish
(Jonah 1-3)

Lesson 2: Good Sheep
(John 10)

Lesson 3: A Big Boat
(Genesis 6)

Lesson 4: Tree Trouble
(Genesis 3)

Lesson 5: Follow Me
(Matthew 4)

Core Concept
I can obey like Jesus.

Scripture Seed
Anyone who has my commands and obeys them loves me.
– John 14:21(NIrV)

Life Lesson
I can listen and obey!

Planting God's Word into children one seed at a time

SCRIPTURE SEED CARDS

Always try to be kind to each other and to everyone else.
1 Thessalonians 5:15 (NIRV)

Always try to be kind to each other and to everyone else.
1 Thessalonians 5:15 (NIRV)

Always try to be kind to each other and to everyone else.
1 Thessalonians 5:15 (NIRV)

1

Always try to be kind to each other and to everyone else.
1 Thessalonians 5:15 (NIRV)

Always try to be kind to each other and to everyone else.
1 Thessalonians 5:15 (NIRV)

Always try to be kind to each other and to everyone else.
1 Thessalonians 5:15 (NIRV)

Forgive each other, just as God forgave you because of what Christ has done.
Ephesians 4:32 (NIRV)

Forgive each other, just as God forgave you because of what Christ has done.
Ephesians 4:32 (NIRV)

Forgive each other, just as God forgave you because of what Christ has done.
Ephesians 4:32 (NIRV)

2

Forgive each other, just as God forgave you because of what Christ has done.
Ephesians 4:32 (NIRV)

Forgive each other, just as God forgave you because of what Christ has done.
Ephesians 4:32 (NIRV)

Forgive each other, just as God forgave you because of what Christ has done.
Ephesians 4:32 (NIRV)

Anyone who has my commands and obeys them loves me.

John 14:21 (NIRV)

Anyone who has my commands and obeys them loves me.

John 14:21 (NIRV)

Anyone who has my commands and obeys them loves me.

John 14:21 (NIRV)

3

Anyone who has my commands and obeys them loves me.

John 14:21 (NIRV)

Anyone who has my commands and obeys them loves me.

John 14:21 (NIRV)

Anyone who has my commands and obeys them loves me.

John 14:21 (NIRV)

ACTIVITY PAGES

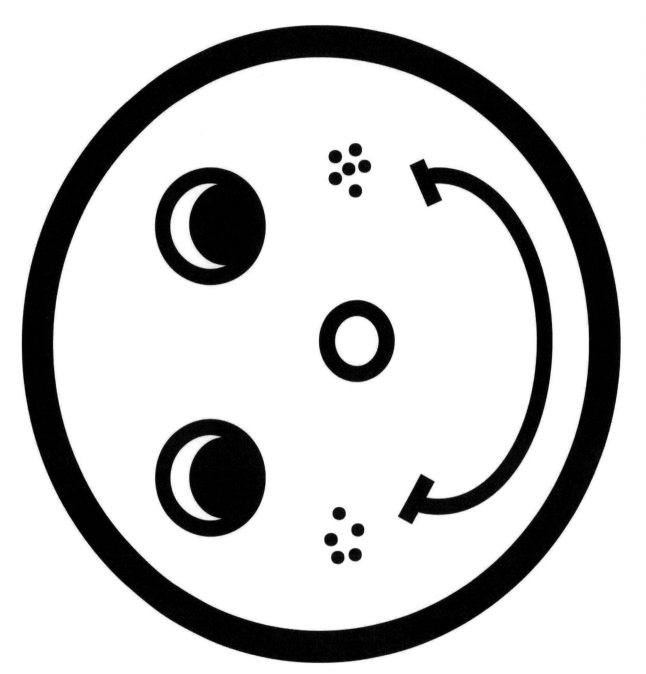

I am kind

I am kind

Print onto cardstock and cut out eyes for mask.

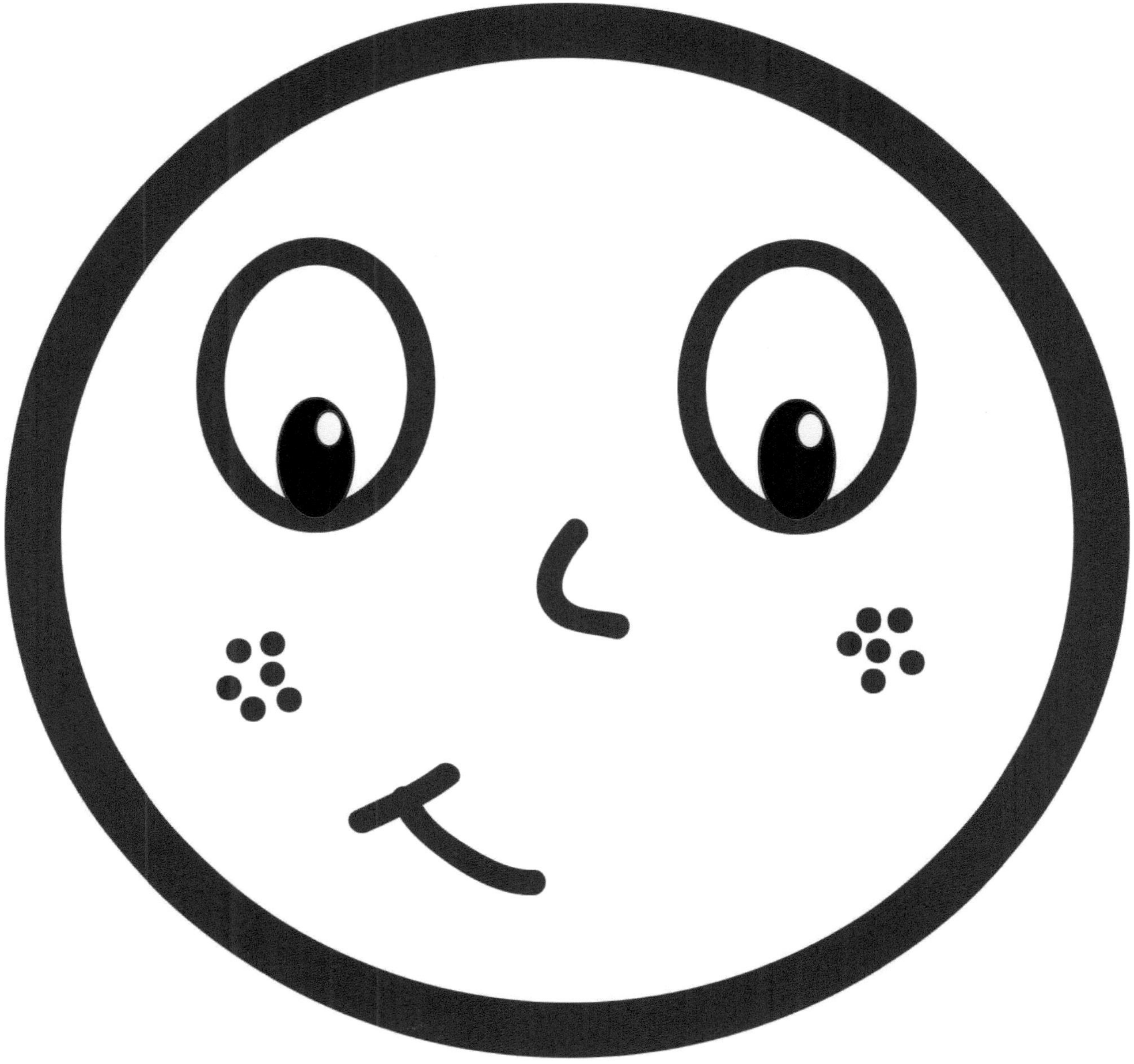

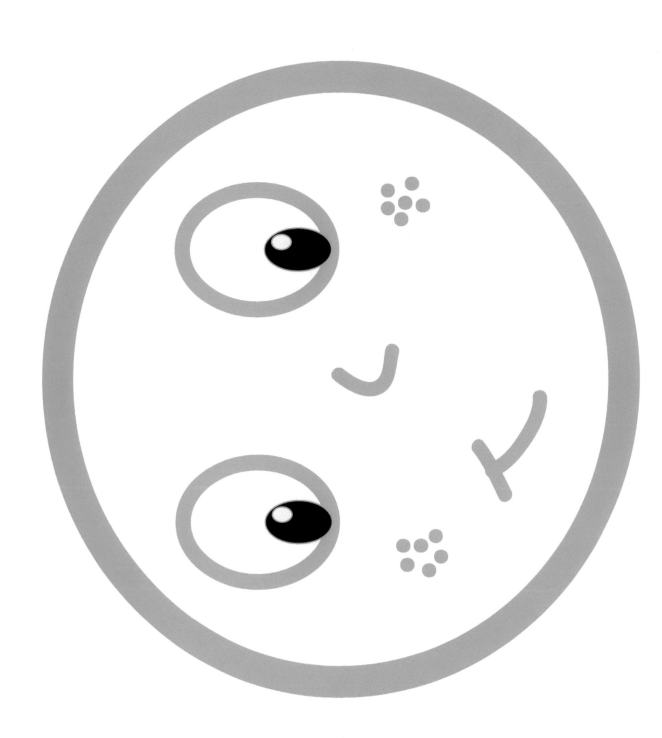

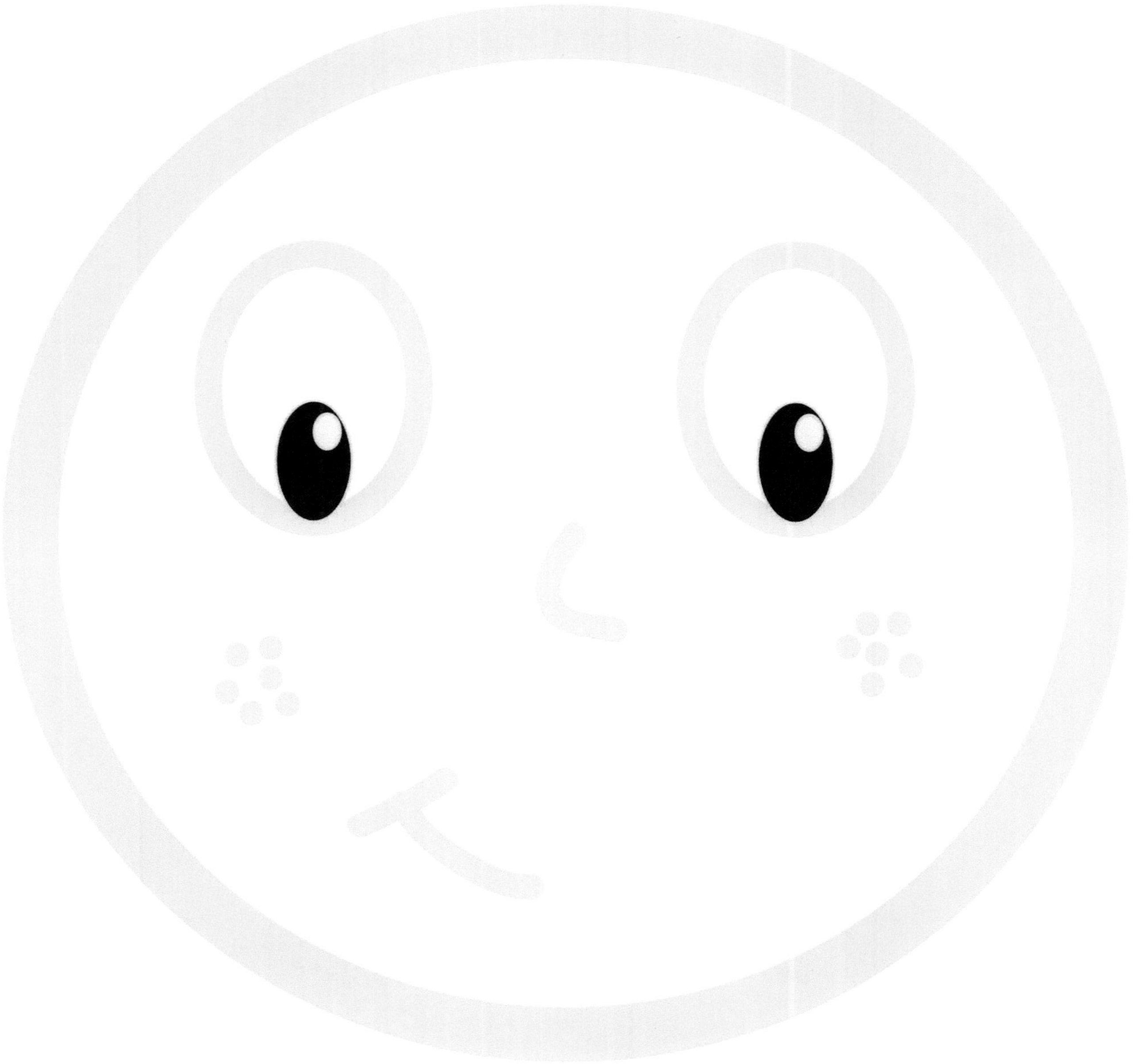

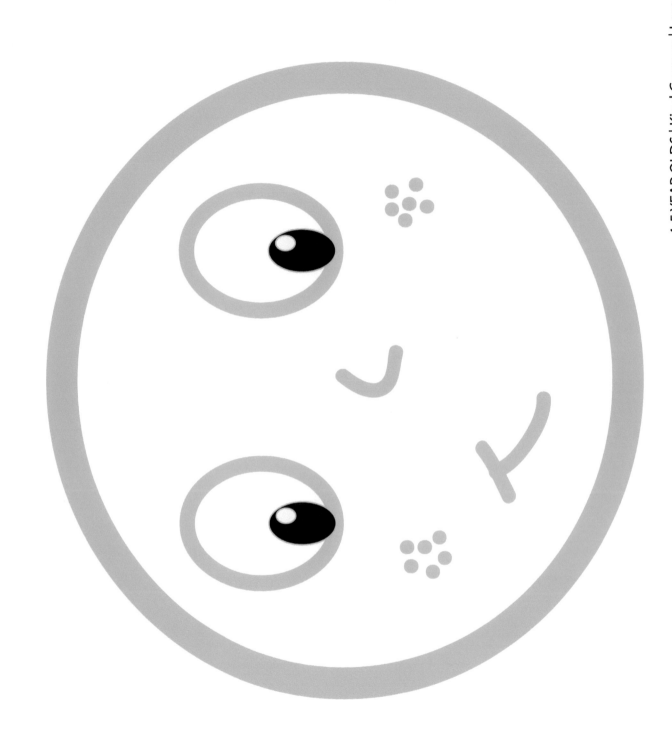

2-5 YEAR OLDS | Kind all the Time | Lesson 1.1-1.4

Laminate for monthly use. Cut out minute & hour hands and fasten to clock with fastener.

Copy onto cardstock.
Cut out crown and staple ends together.

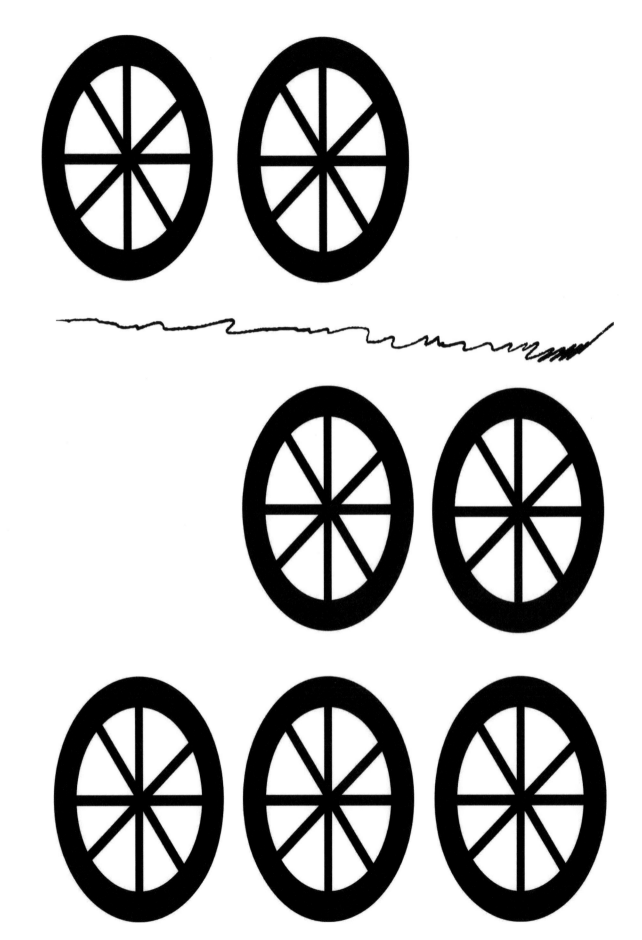

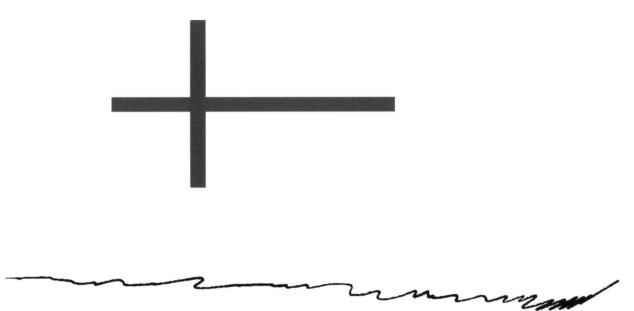

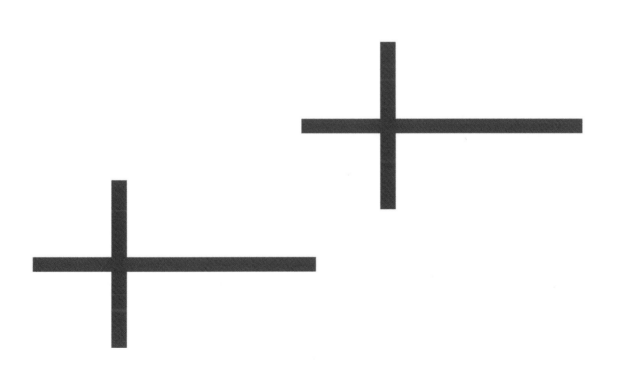

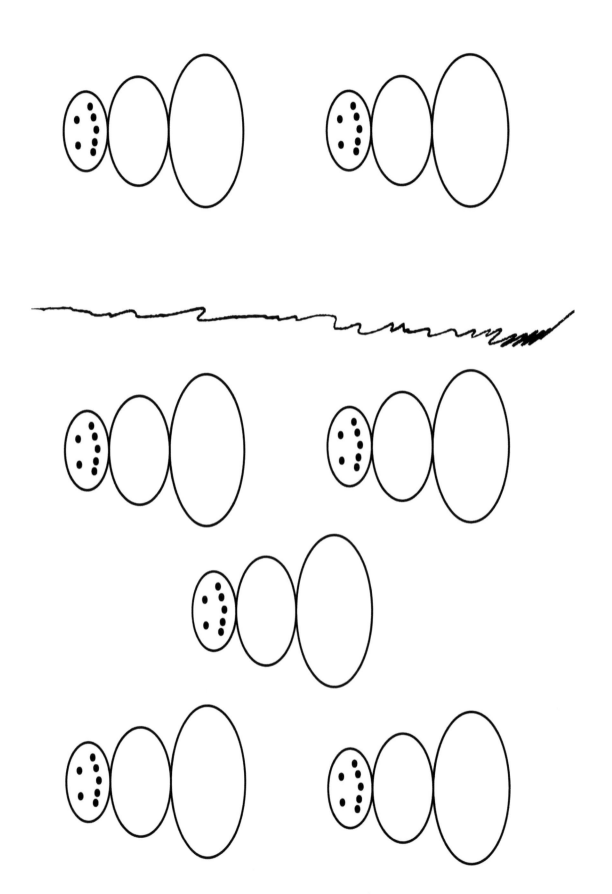

4-5 YEAR OLDS | Lots & Little | Lesson 1.4

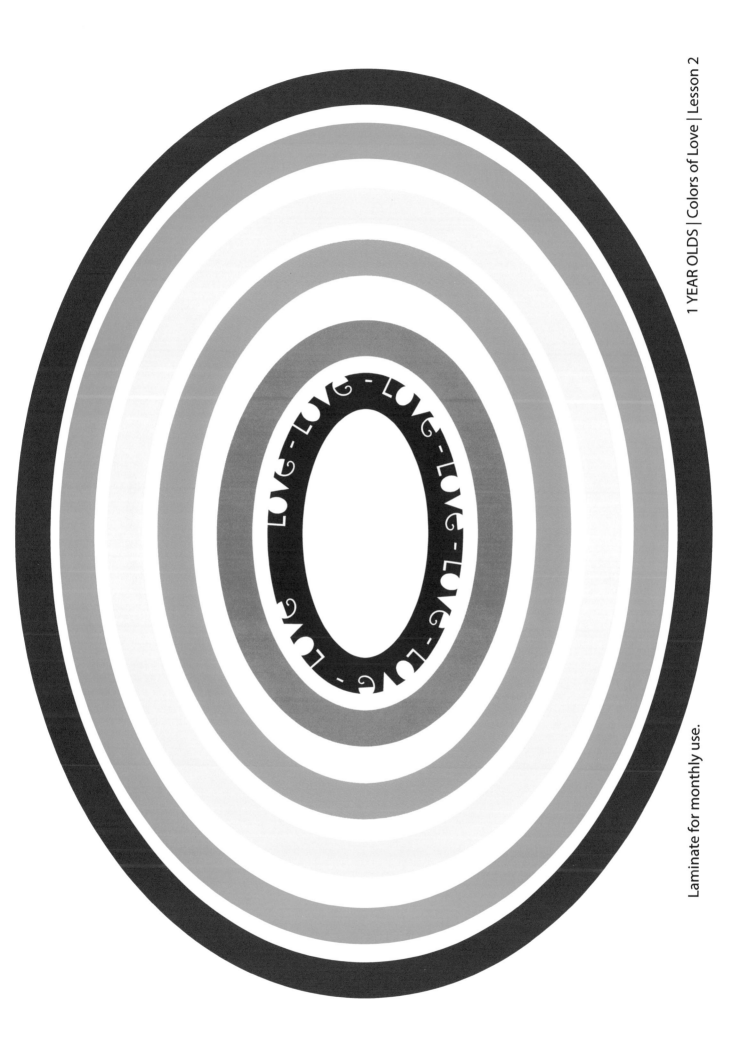

LOVE - LOVE - LOVE - LOVE - LOVE - LOVE - LOVE - LOVE - LOVE

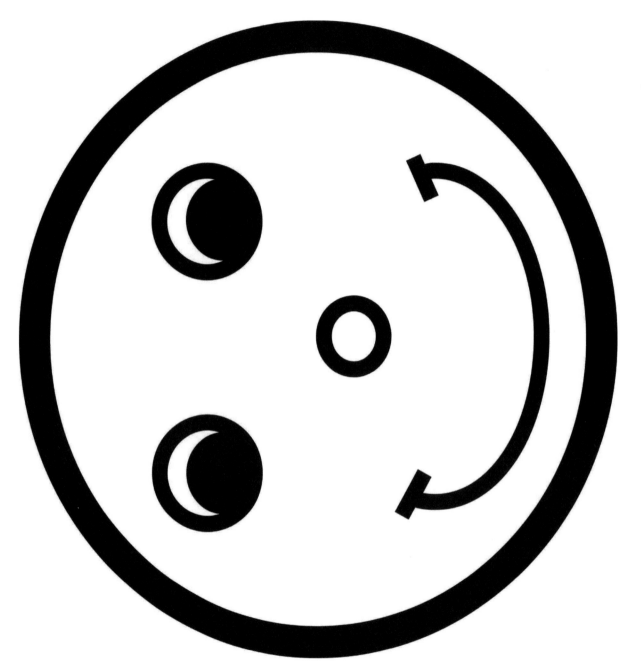

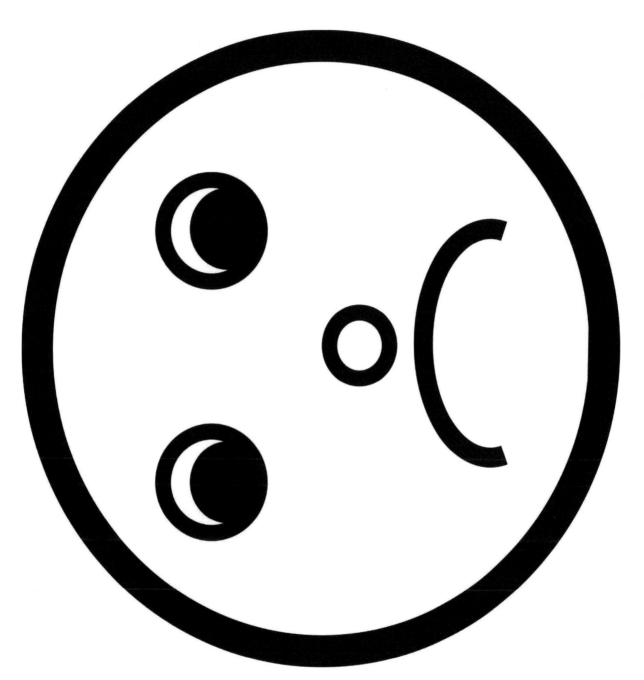

Thursday

Sunday

Friday

Wednesday

Saturday

Tuesday

Monday

EVERYDAY FORGIVER

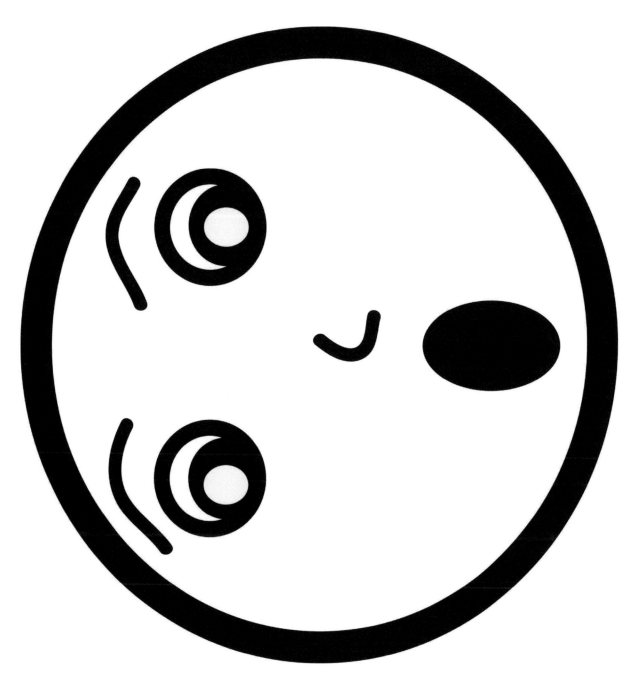

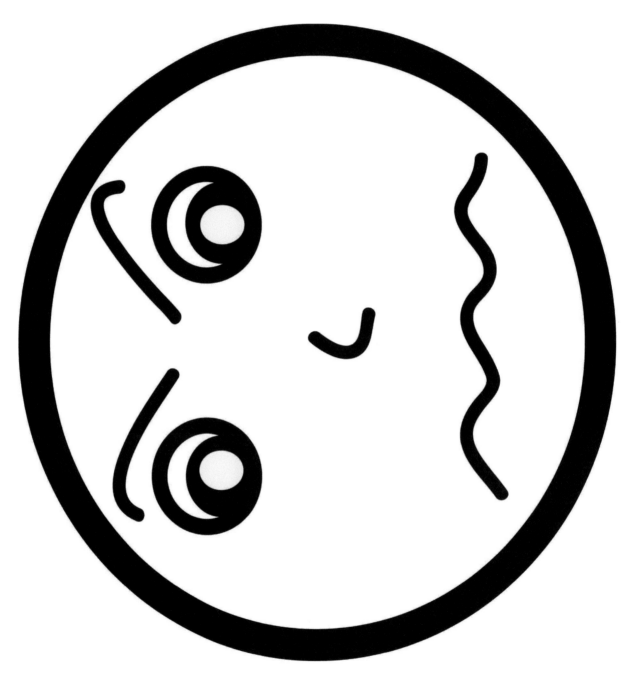

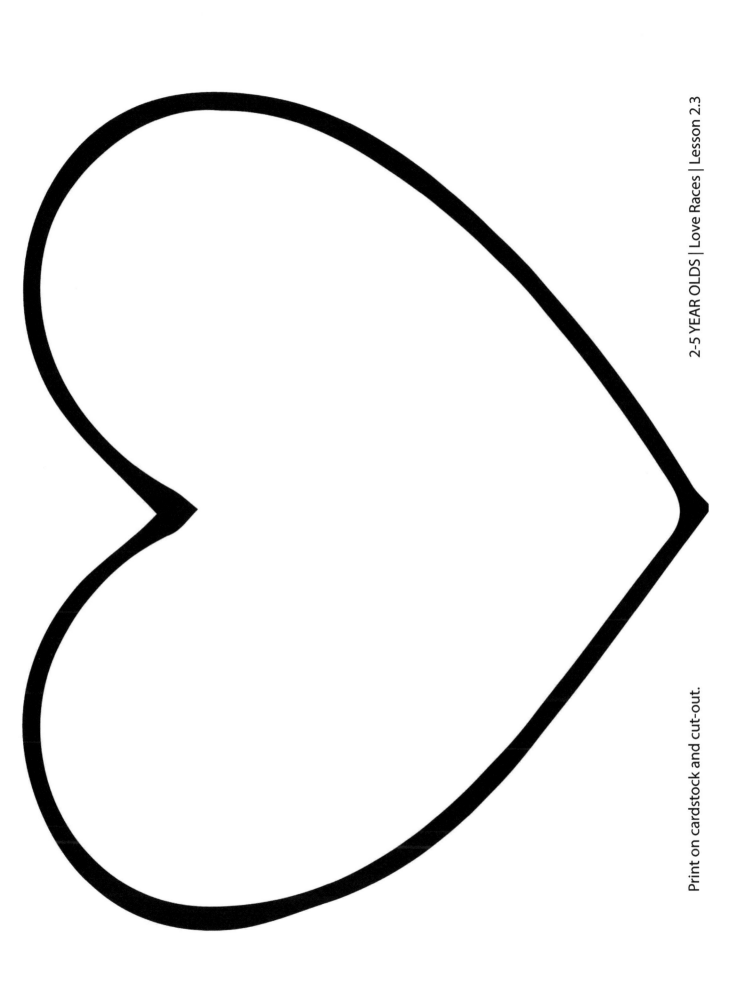

Print on cardstock and cut-out.

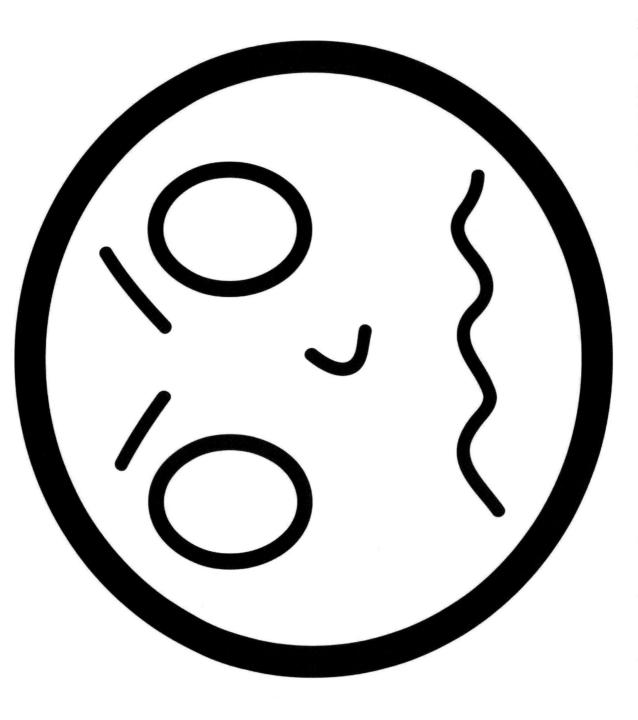

Cut out eyes for mean face mask.

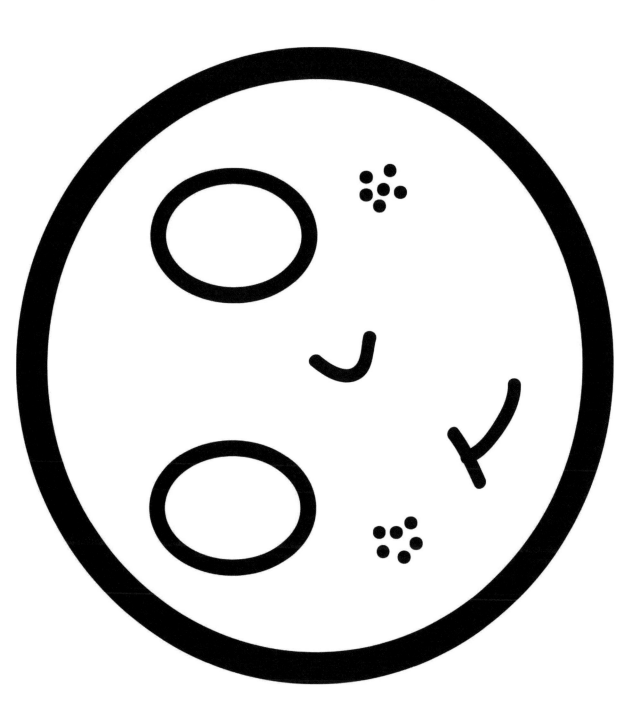

Cut out eyes for happy face mask.

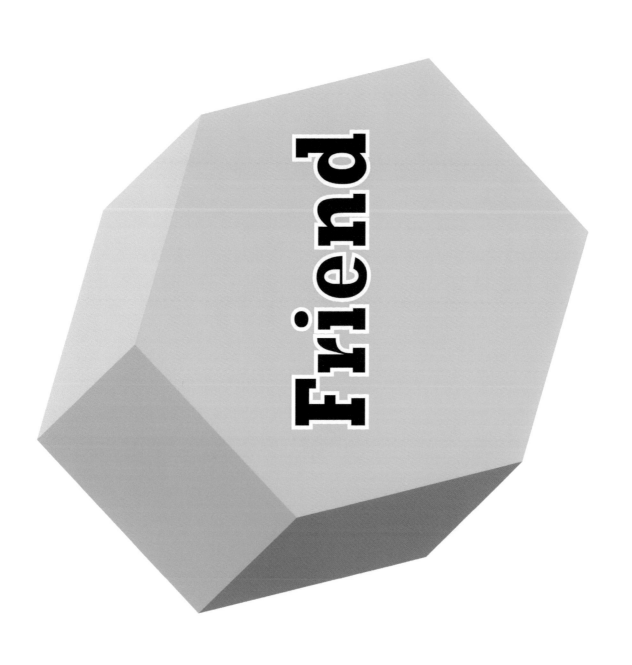

Friend

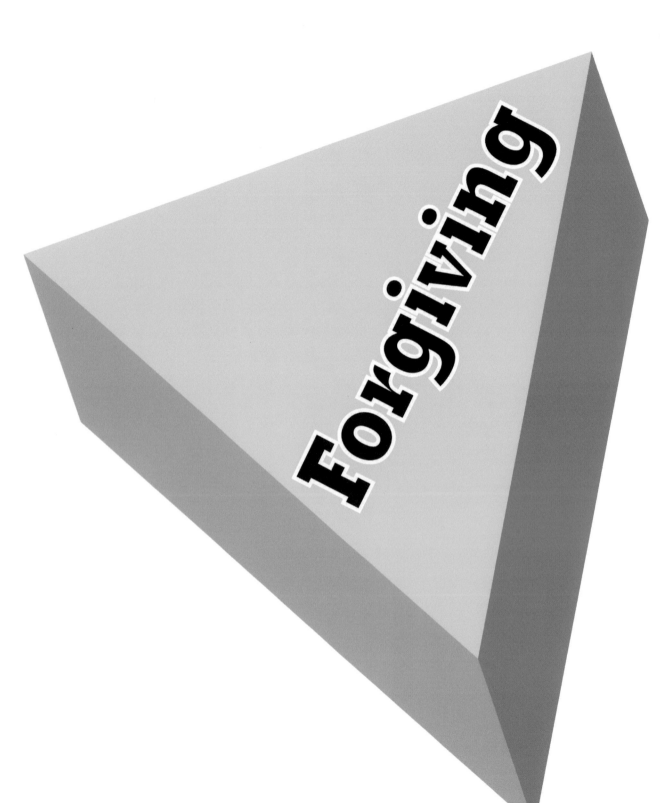

Forgiving

Loving

Obedient

Kind

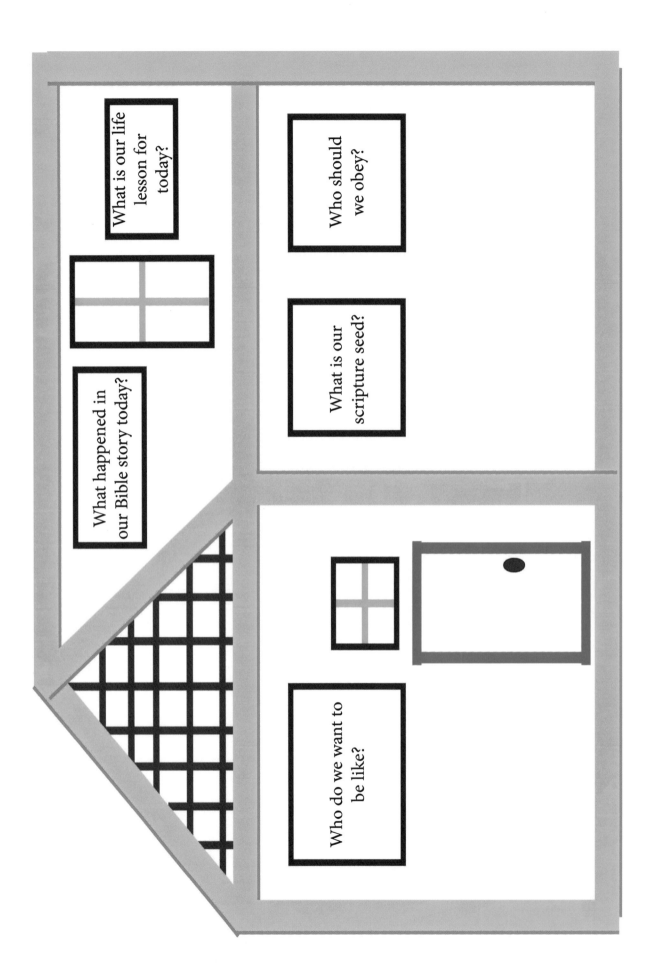

What is our life lesson for today?

What happened in our Bible story today?

Who should we obey?

What is our scripture seed?

Who do we want to be like?

Laminate for monthly use.

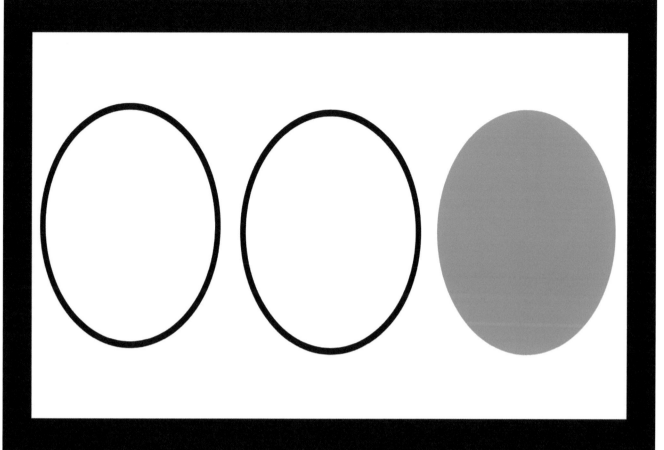

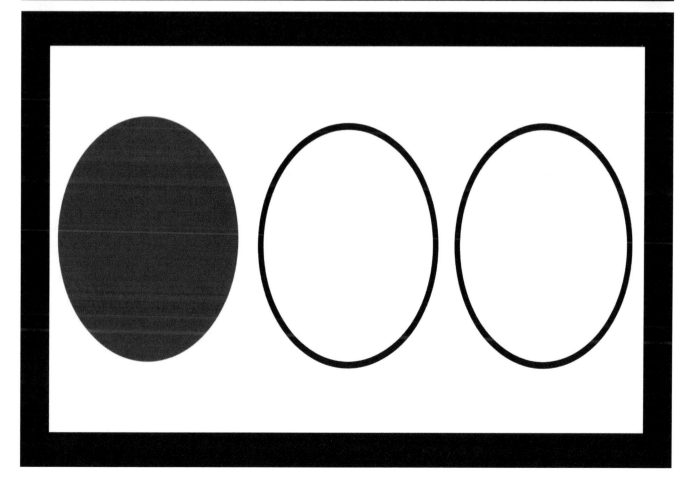

MARCH 3 STEPS FORWARD

HOP 2 STEPS TO THE RIGHT

RAISE YOUR ARMS 2 TIMES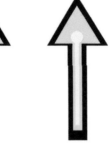

SKIP 5 STEPS TO THE LEFT

TIPTOE 4 STEPS FORWARD

JUMP 5 TIMES

YOU HAVE FOUND THE STICKERS!

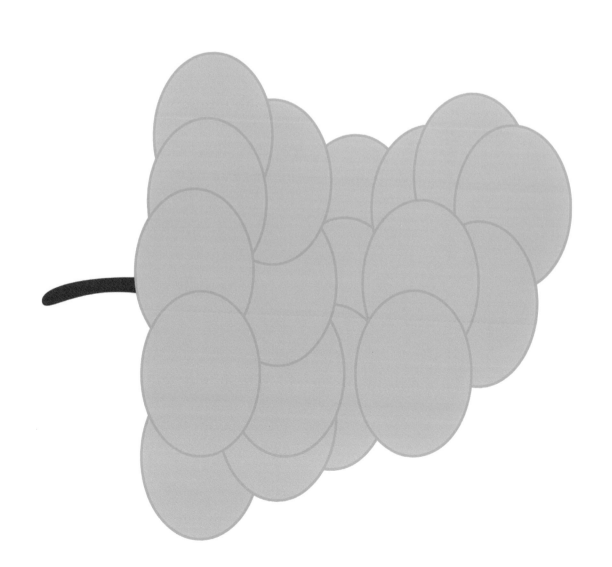

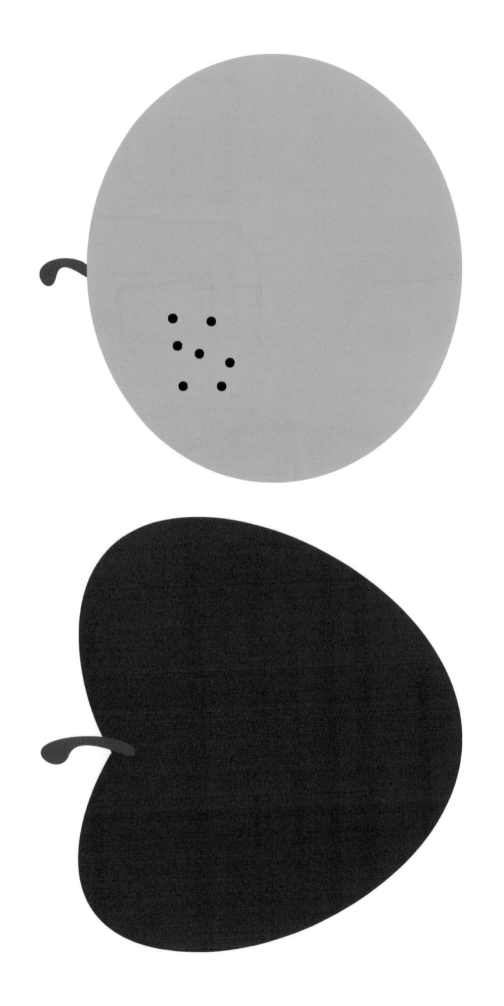

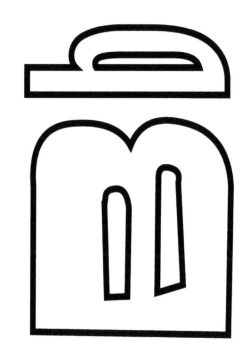

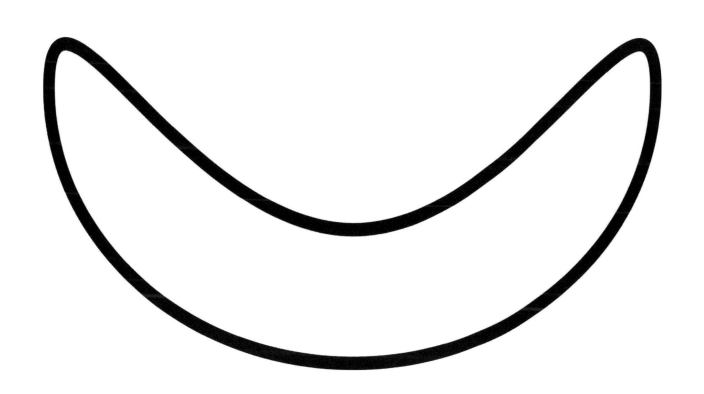

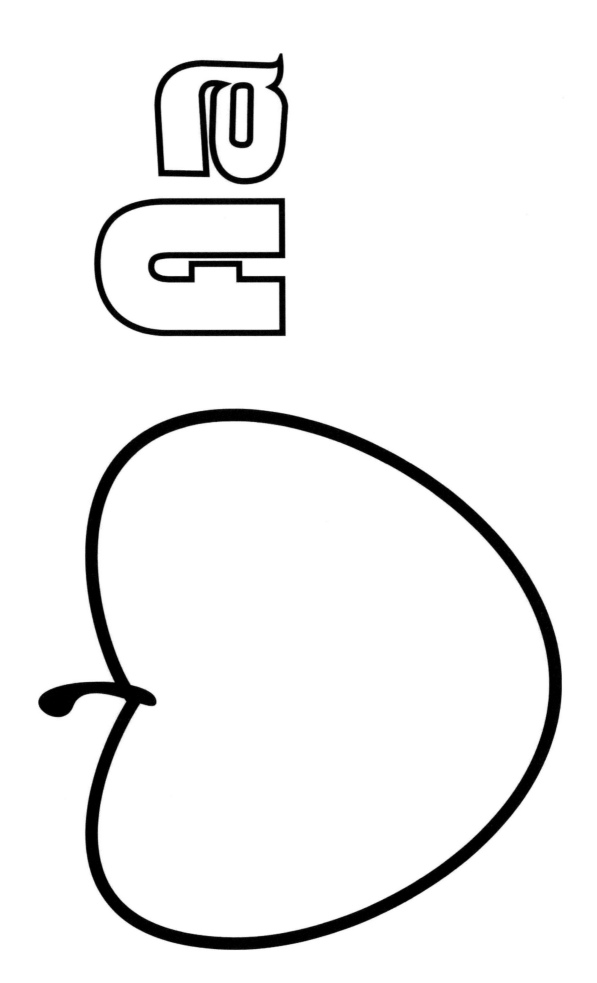

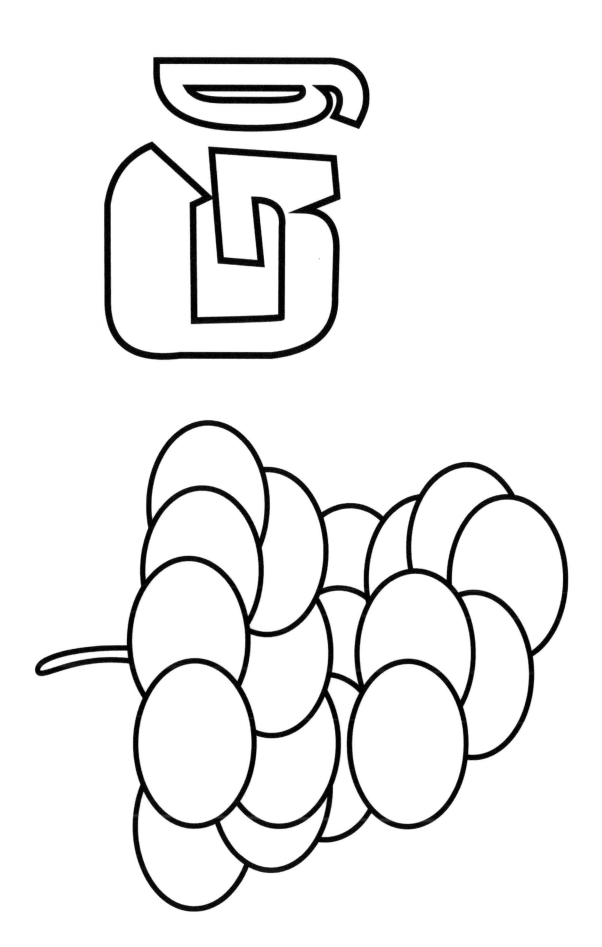

CPSIA information can be obtained
at www.ICGtesting.com
Printed in the USA
LVIC04n0039130614
389884LV00006B/8